# THE
# CURTAIN SKETCH
# BOOK

# THE CURTAIN SKETCH BOOK

*by Wendy Baker*

THE OLD MALTHOUSE, HAM, MARLBOROUGH, SN8 3RB, UNITED KINGDOM
Telephone  01488 66 8989          Fax: 01488 66 8818

Wendy Baker's
Interior Design team
and
Curtain Making Services

The Old Malthouse
Ham
Marlborough
Wiltshire SN8 3RB
Telephone   01488 66 8989
Fax:          01488 66 8818

Other Books by Wendy Baker

# THE BED SKETCH BOOK

First published in 1994 in the
original version by Deco Books
Second printing 1966

Published 1997 by Curtain Sketch Book

ISBN 2–940085–01–3

Printed and bound in Great Britain by
Redwood Books, Trowbridge, Wiltshire

3  4  5  6  7  8  9  /  02  01  00  99  98  97

# CONTENTS

# HOW TO GET THE BEST OUT OF YOUR CURTAIN SKETCH BOOK

*There are many hundreds of curtain designs available, and with the combination of different headings, poles, tie backs etc., the prospect of choosing a window treatment can appear quite daunting.*

***Wendy Baker,*** *an International Interior Designer, has produced **"The Curtain Sketch Book"** in order that her clients can choose their curtains from simplified line drawings without any confusion. The concept has been a great success and her book is used by interior designers throughout the world.*

***"The Curtain Sketch Book"*** *shows the most popular designs in clear, easy to understand sketches which enable you to choose your own window dressing in the comfort of your own home, in your own time.*

*Just look through the book to find a design that suits your requirements, be it for a kitchen or a grand ballroom. Now check to see whether the top of the curtain (the heading) is to your liking. If not, turn to the pages that show alternatives and choose a different heading from the one shown. If you require tie backs, follow the same procedure.*

*Make a note of your selection, i.e. Curtain Treatments, page 31, Valances, page 11 No. 10, Tie Backs, page 20 No. 17. Discuss these with your designer or curtain maker who will measure your windows, order the fabric and make up your new curtains. It sometimes helps to see the curtains you have chosen in the colours of your choice. Simply take a photocopy of the sketch and colour.*

# CURTAIN HEADINGS

1

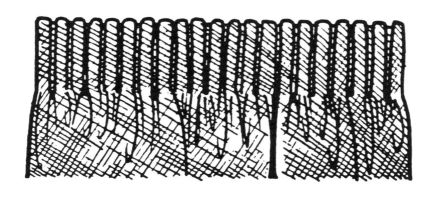

2

3

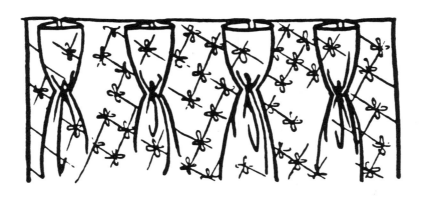

4

5

6

7

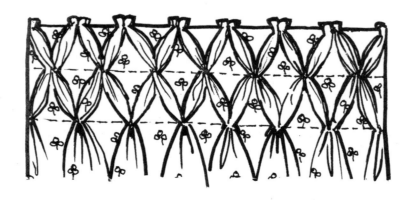

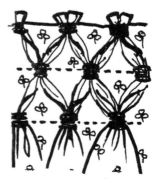

8

# VALANCES

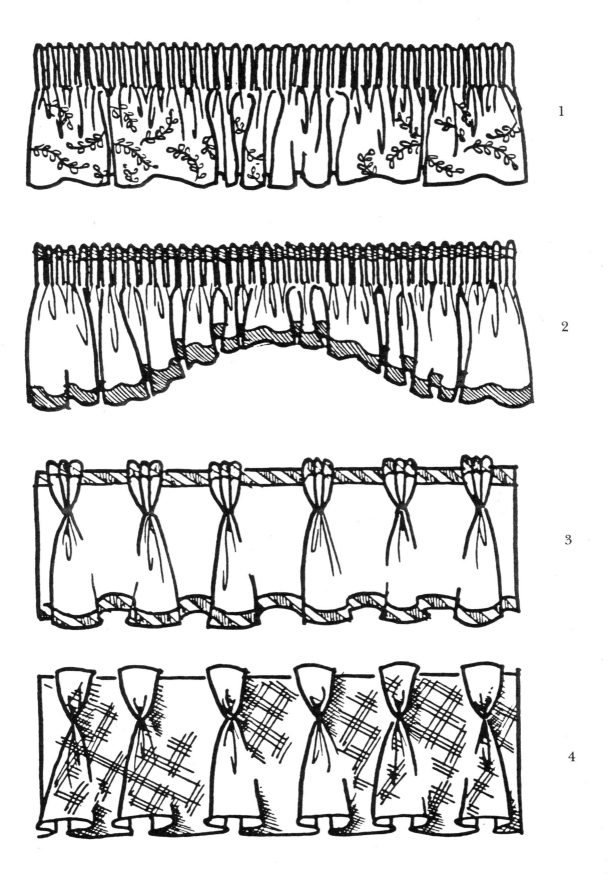

1

2

3

4

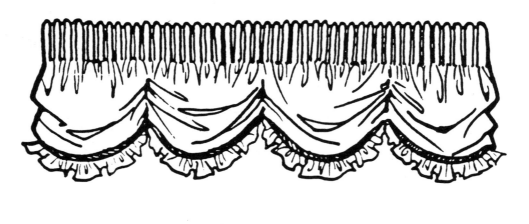

5

6

7

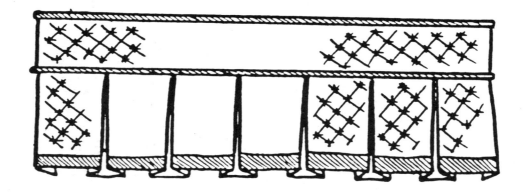

8

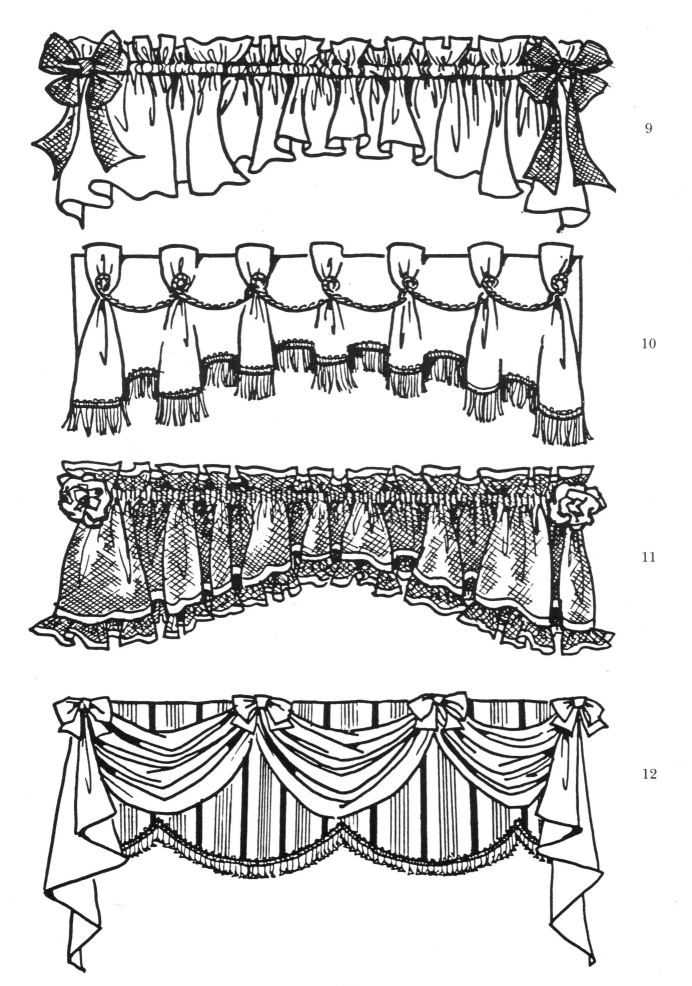

9

10

11

12

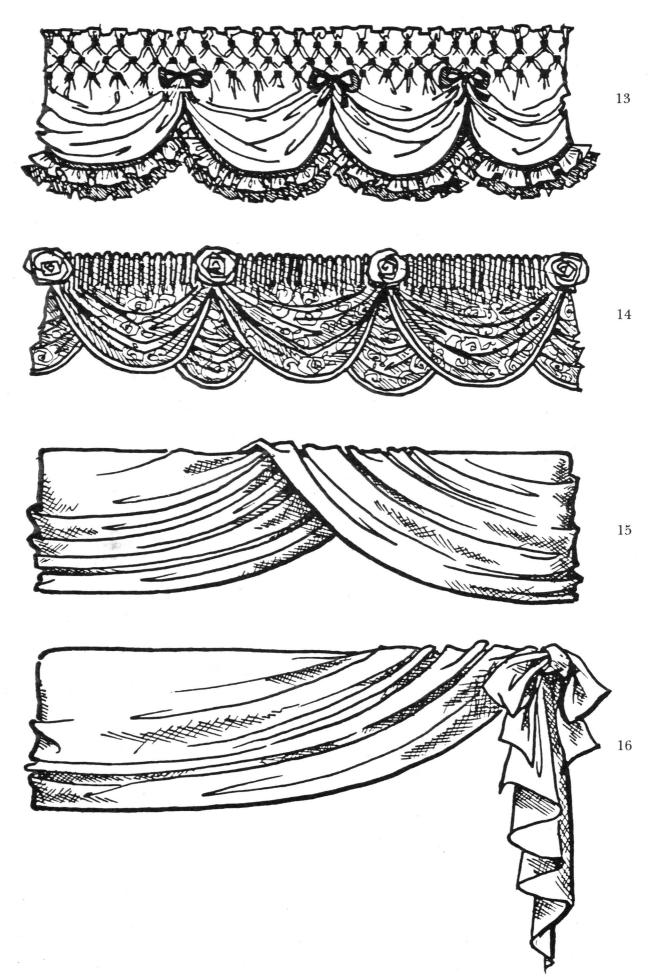

13

14

15

16

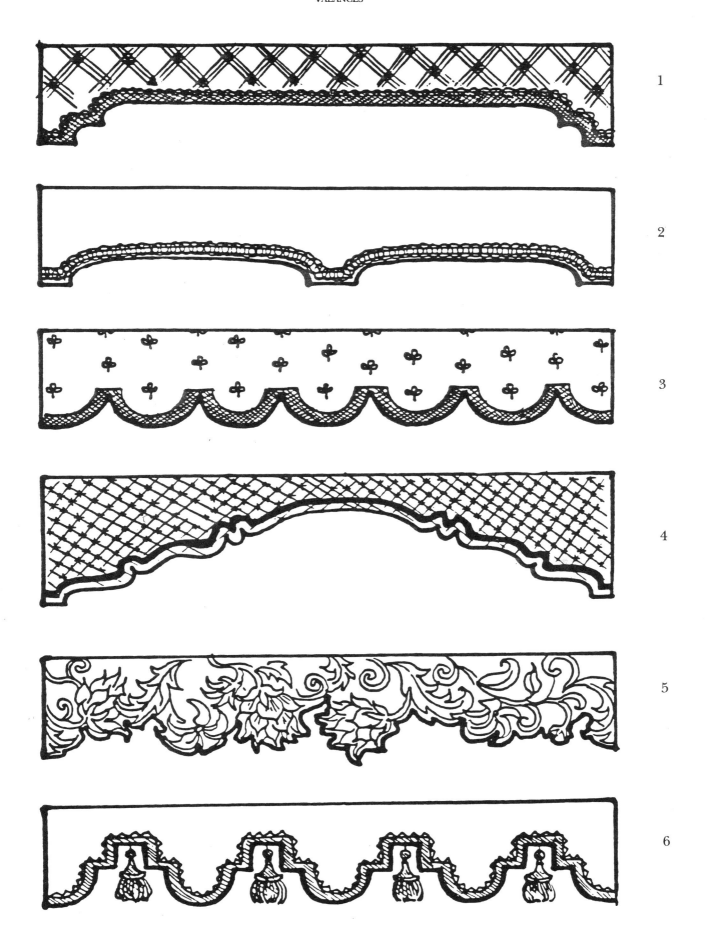

1

2

3

4

5

6

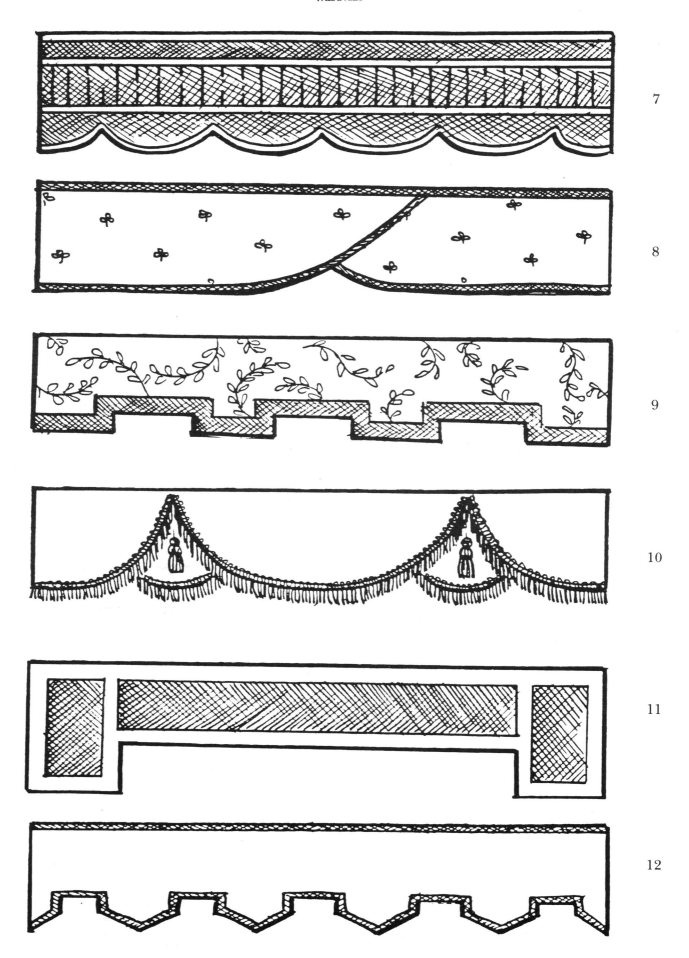

7

8

9

10

11

12

# POLES

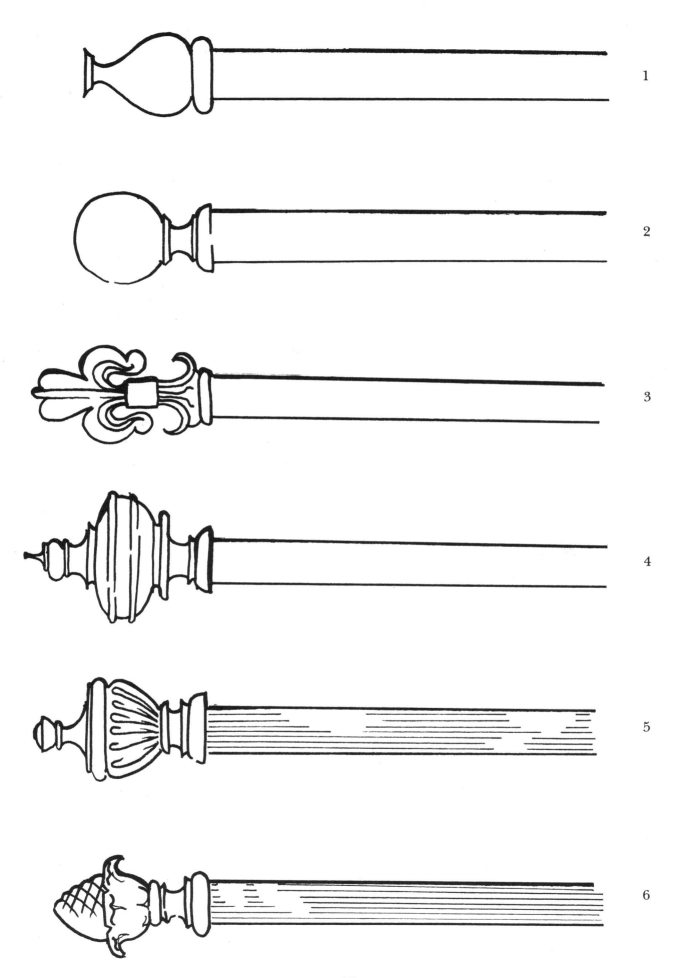

1

2

3

4

5

6

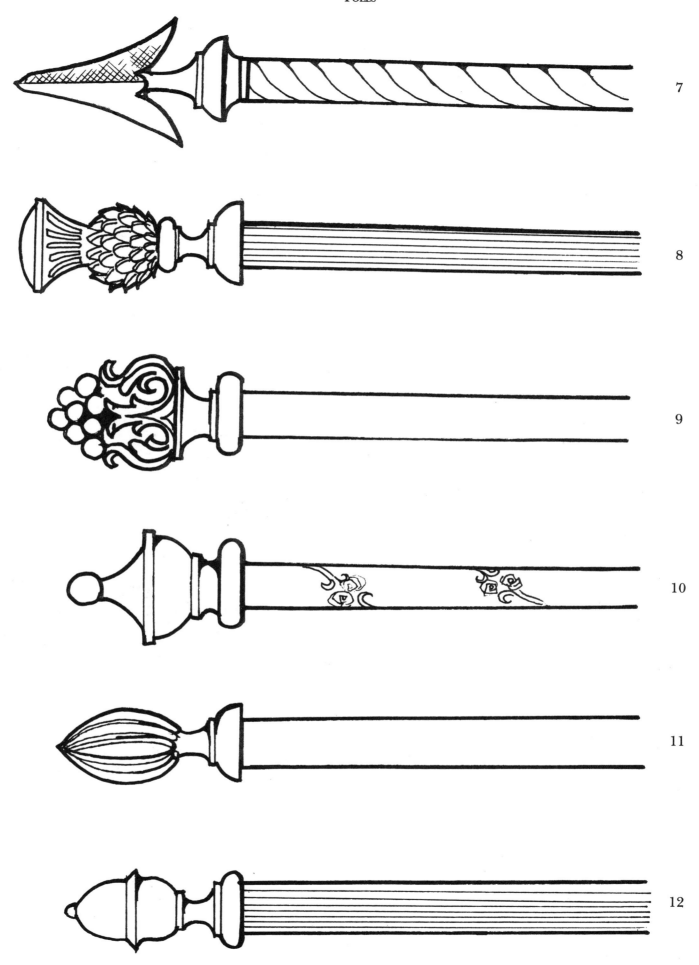

7

8

9

10

11

12

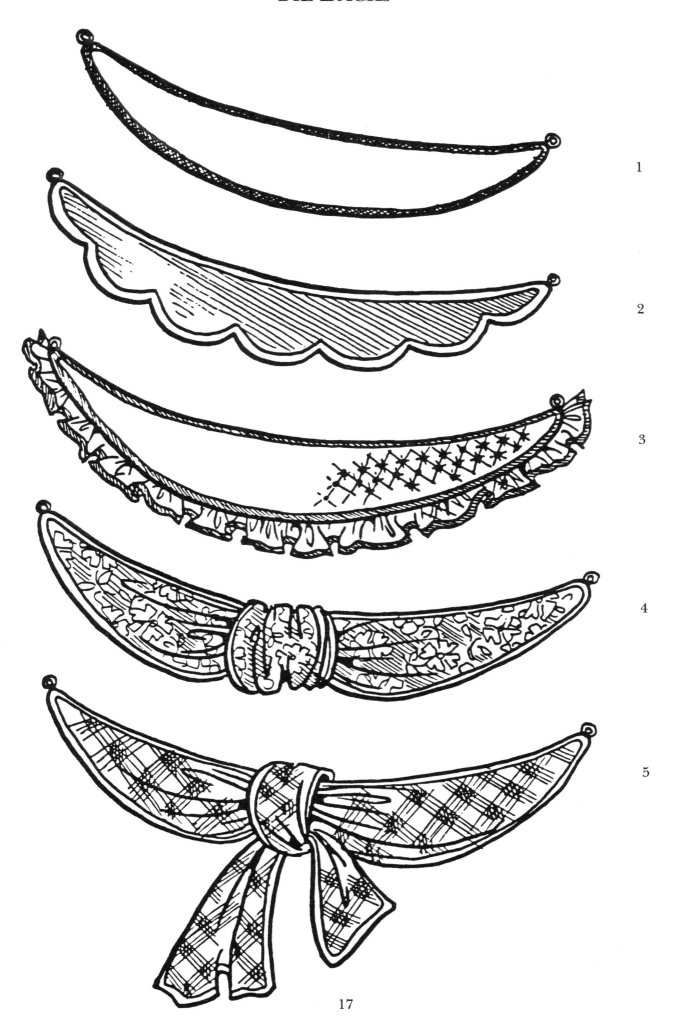

1

2

3

4

5

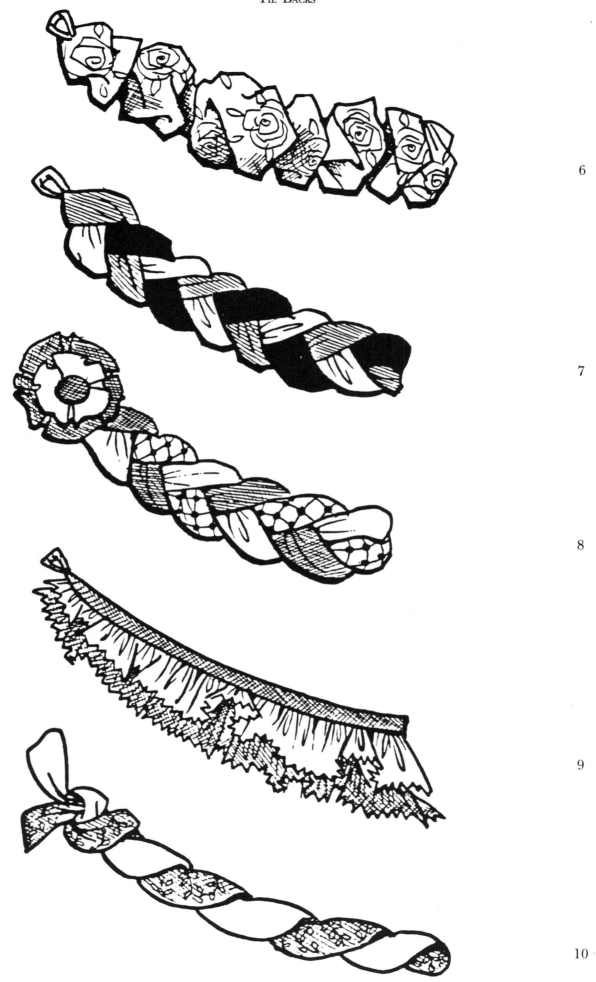

6

7

8

9

10

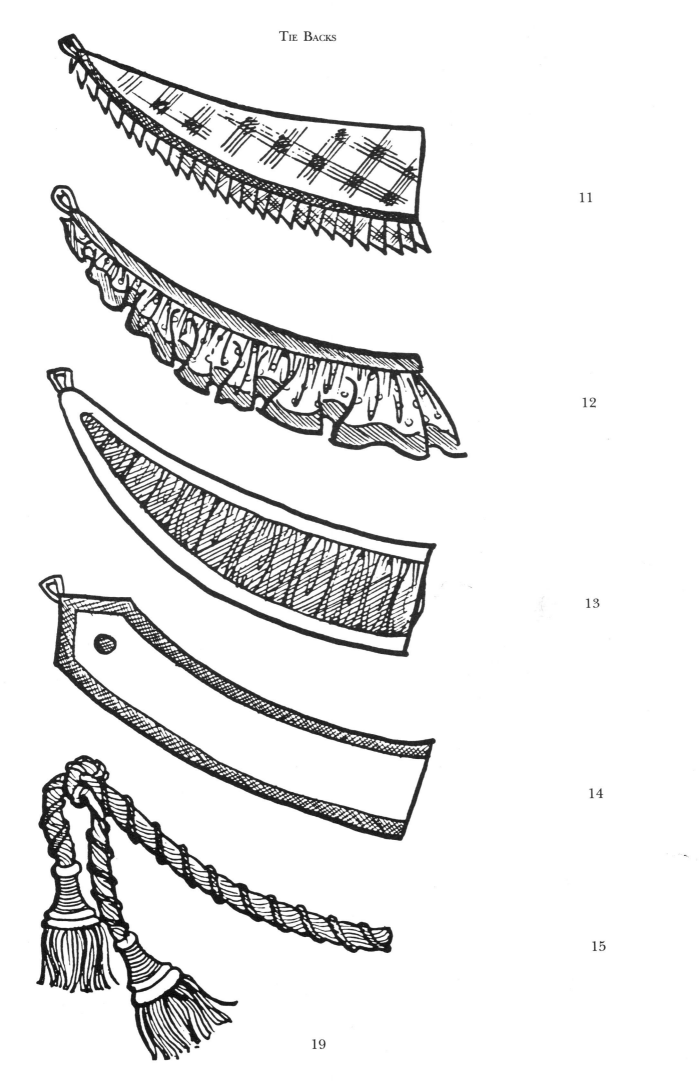

11

12

13

14

15

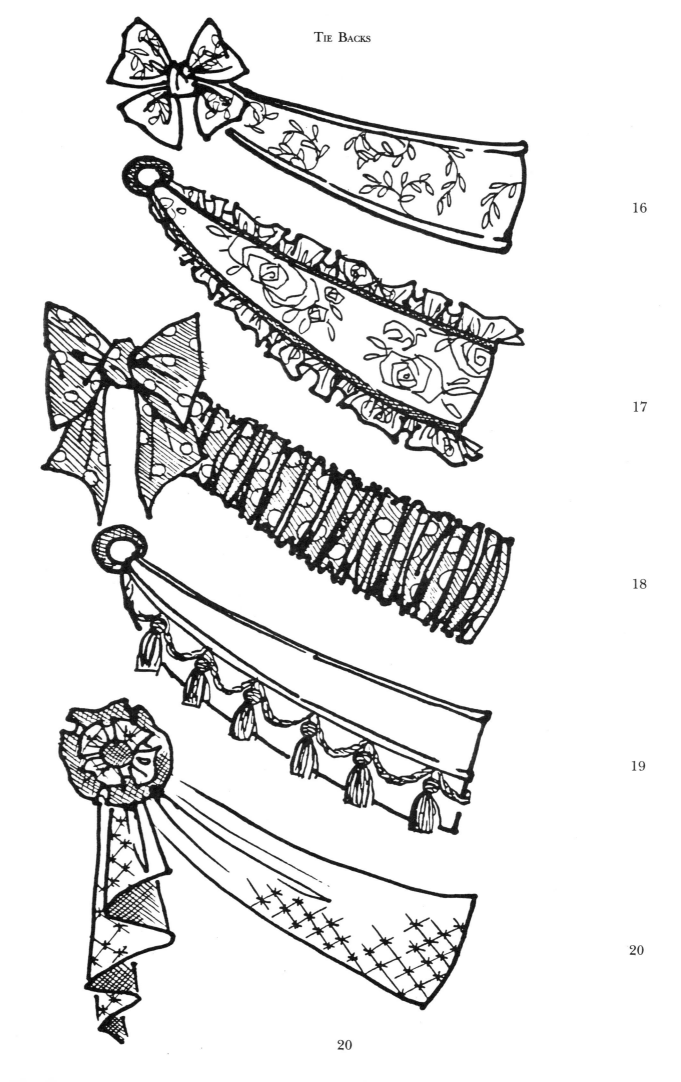

16

17

18

19

20

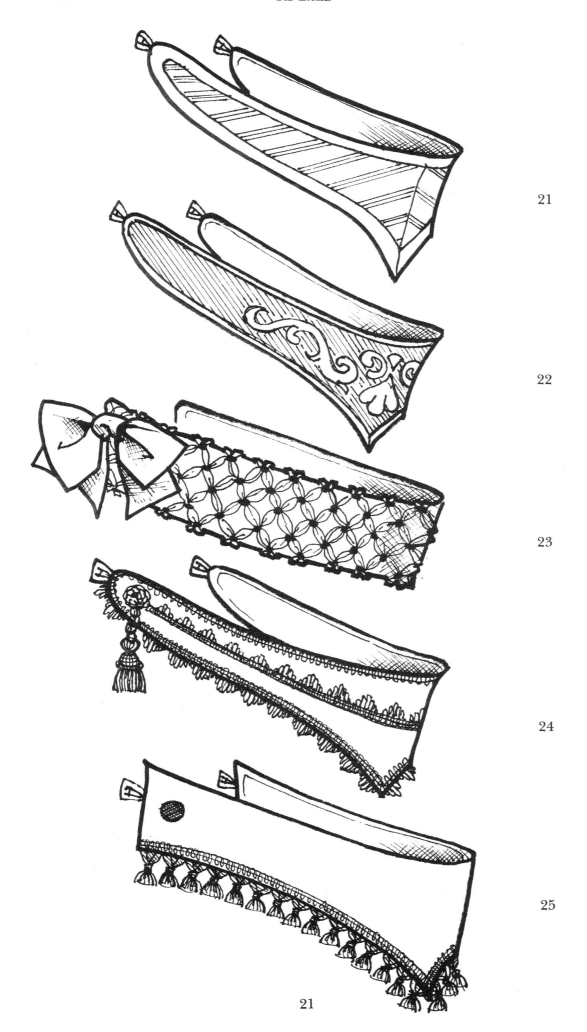

21

22

23

24

25

21

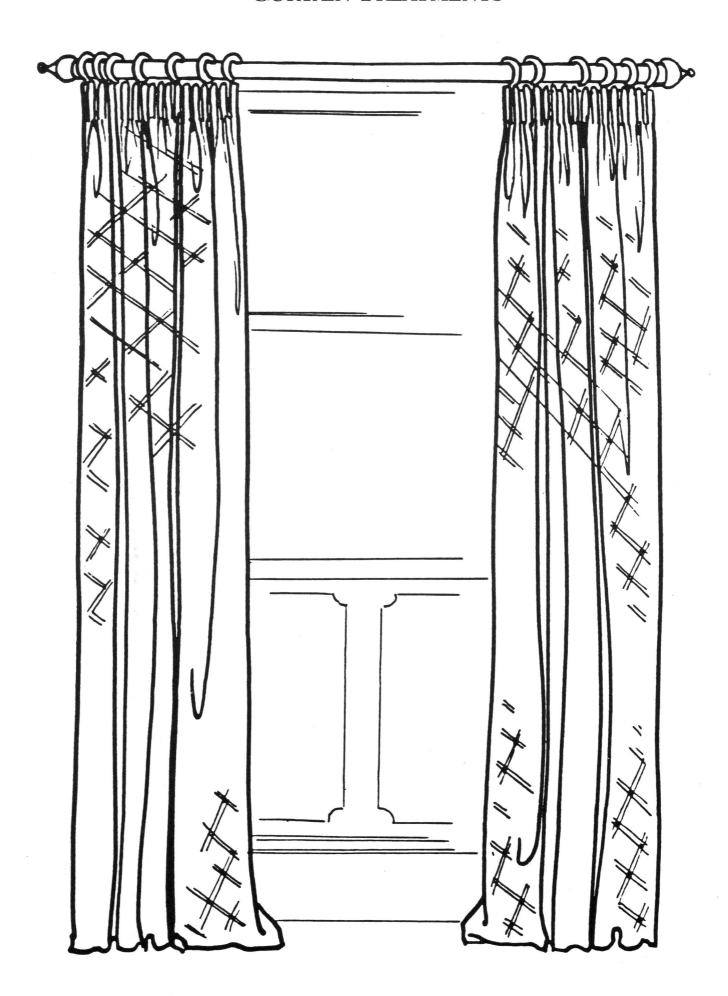

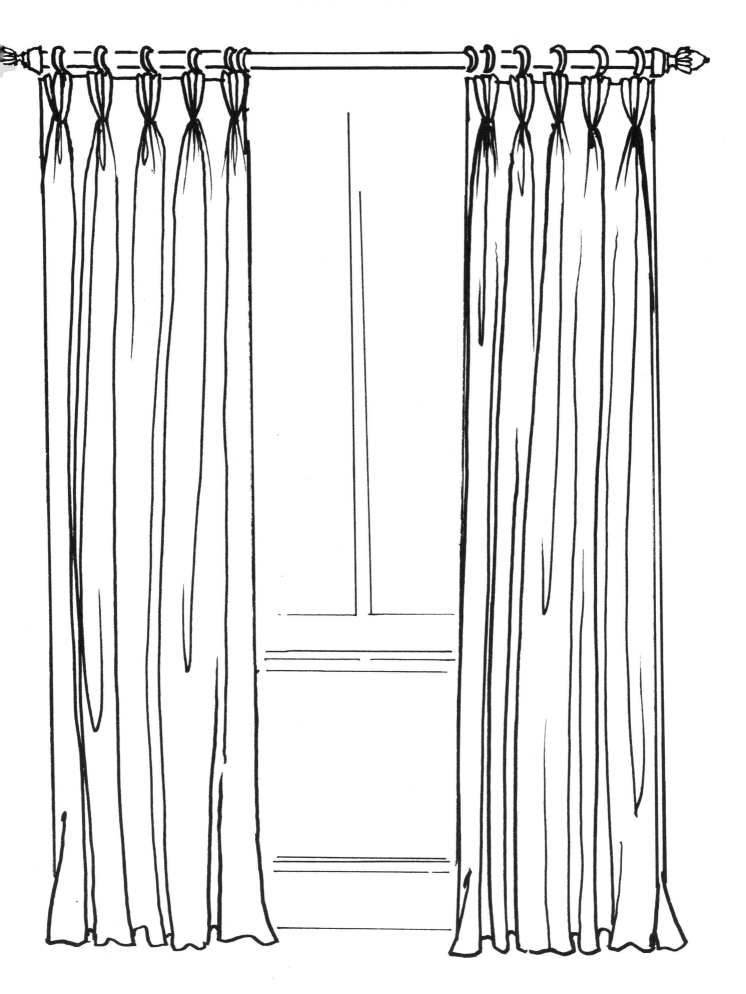

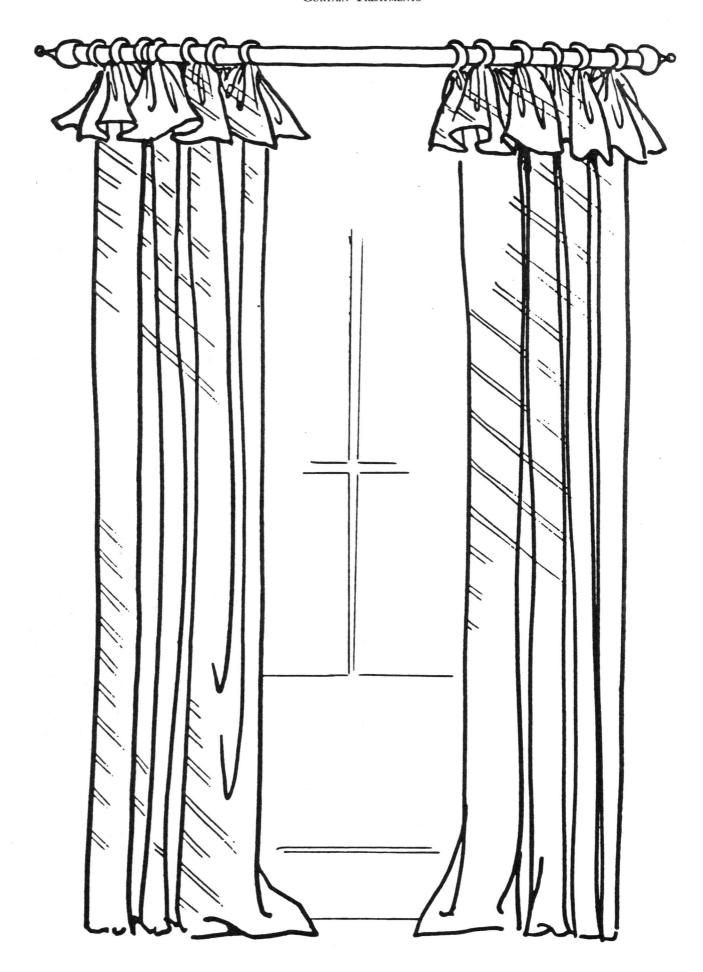

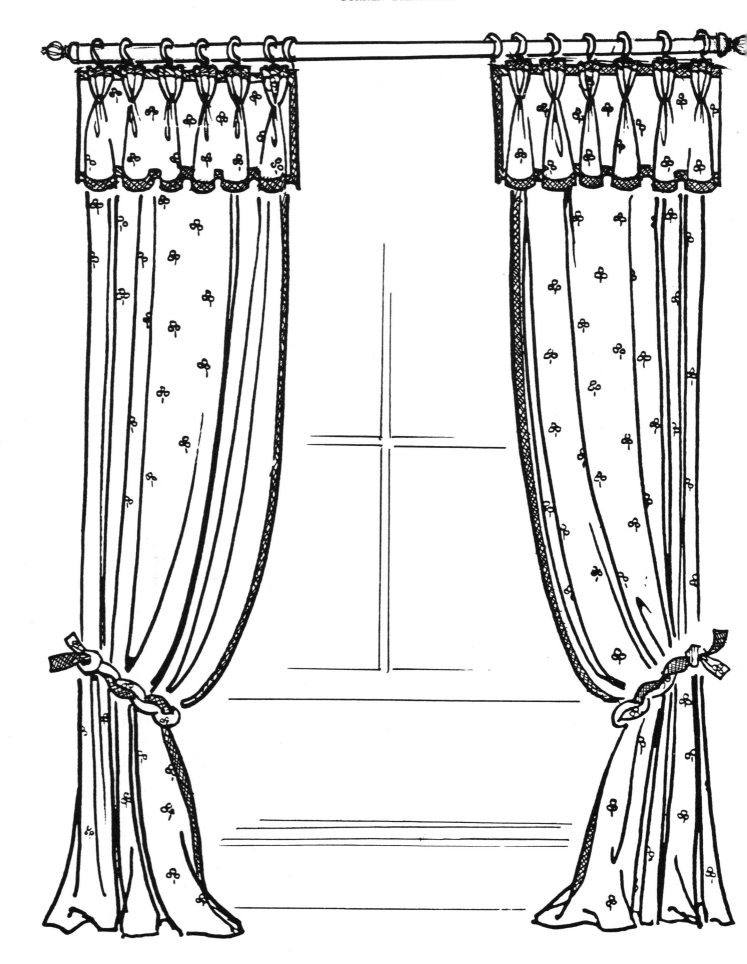

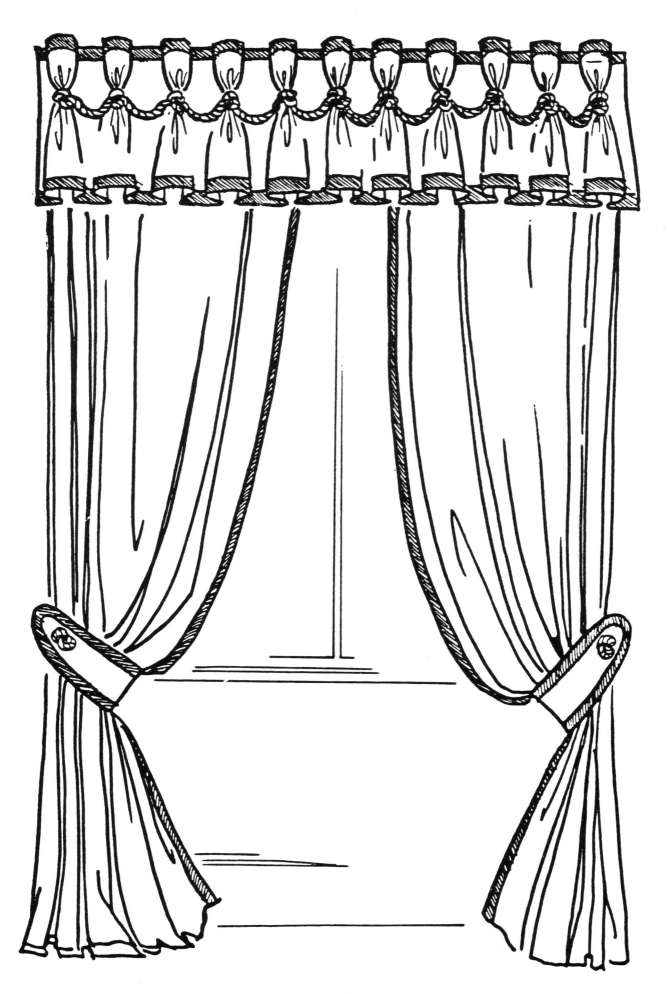

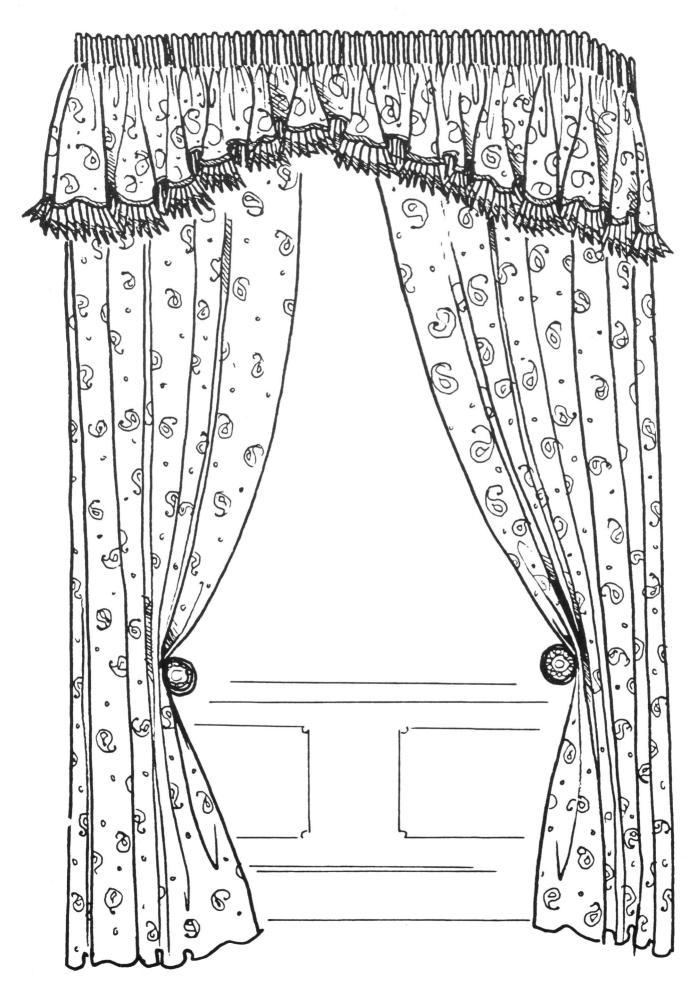

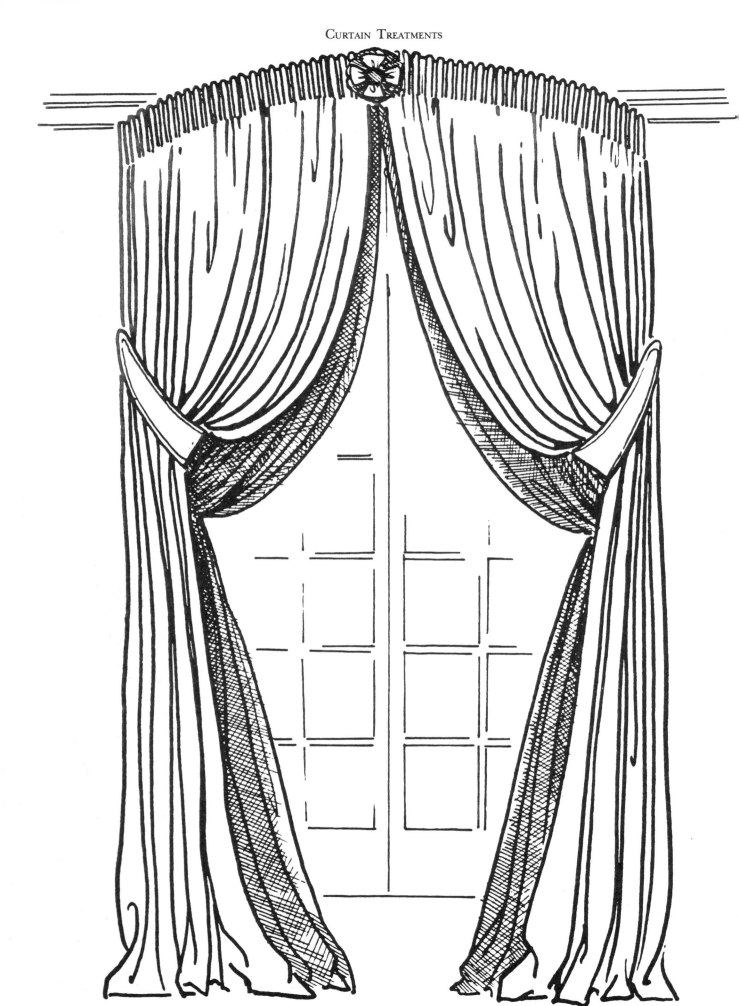

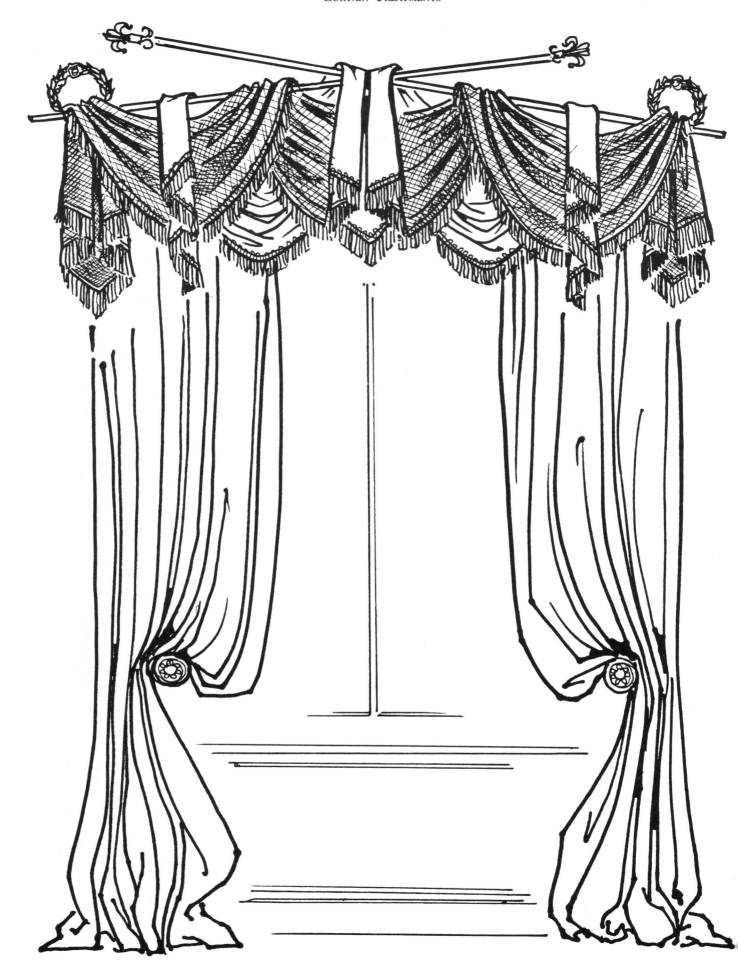

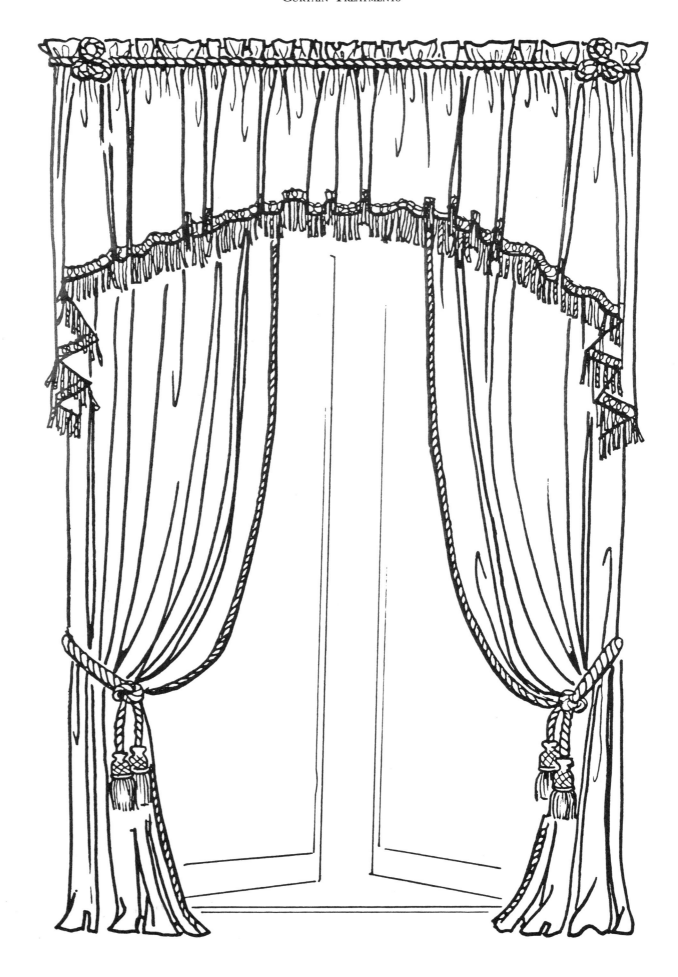

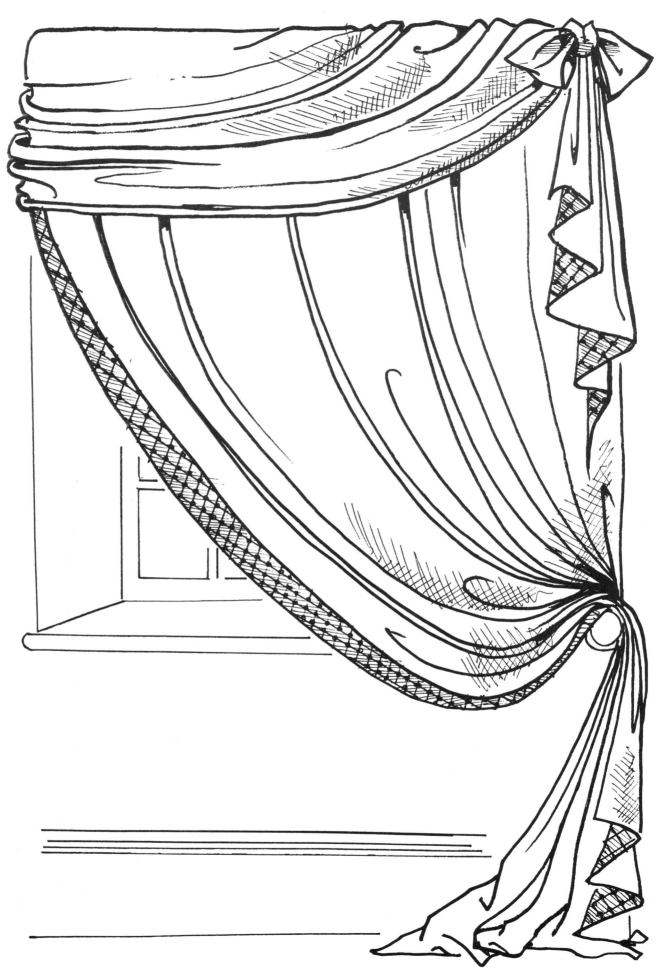

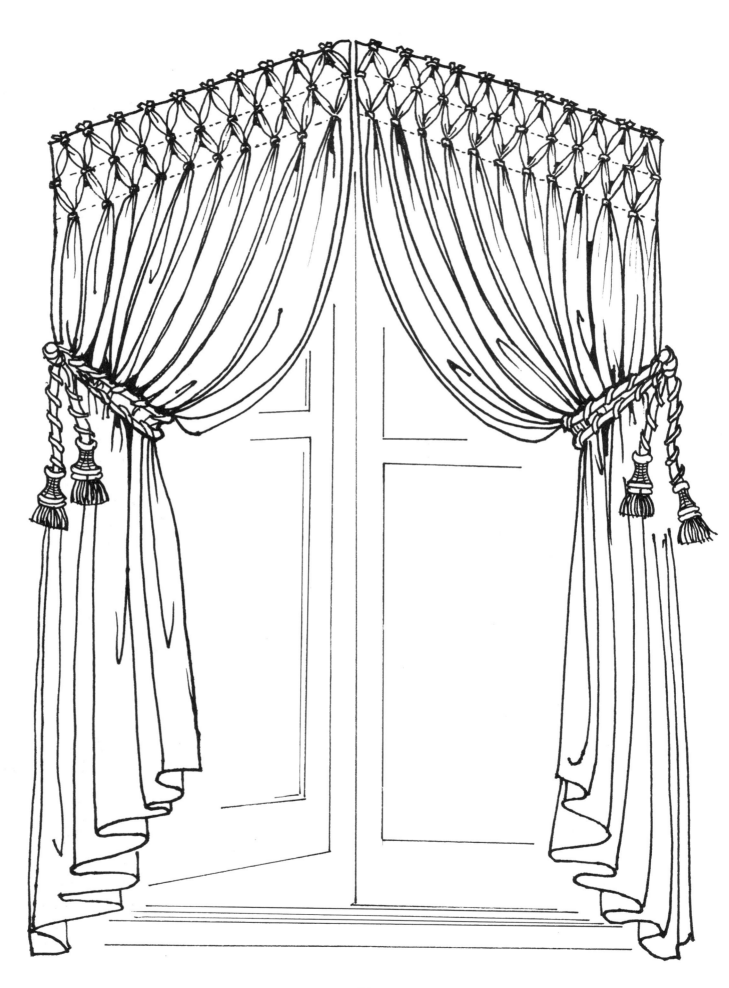

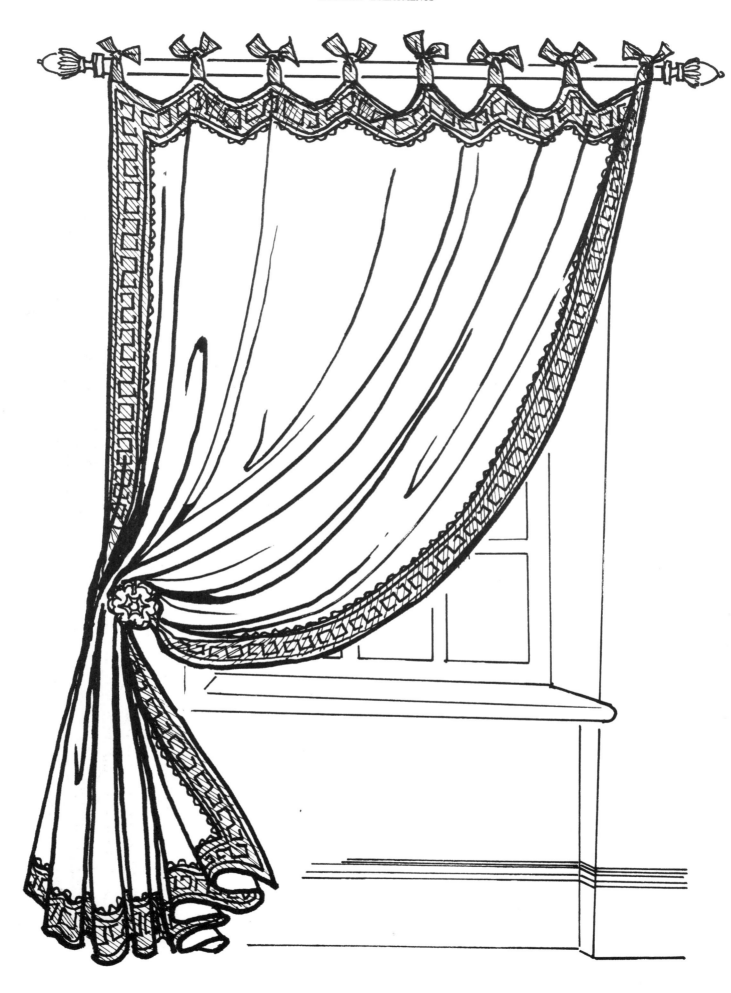

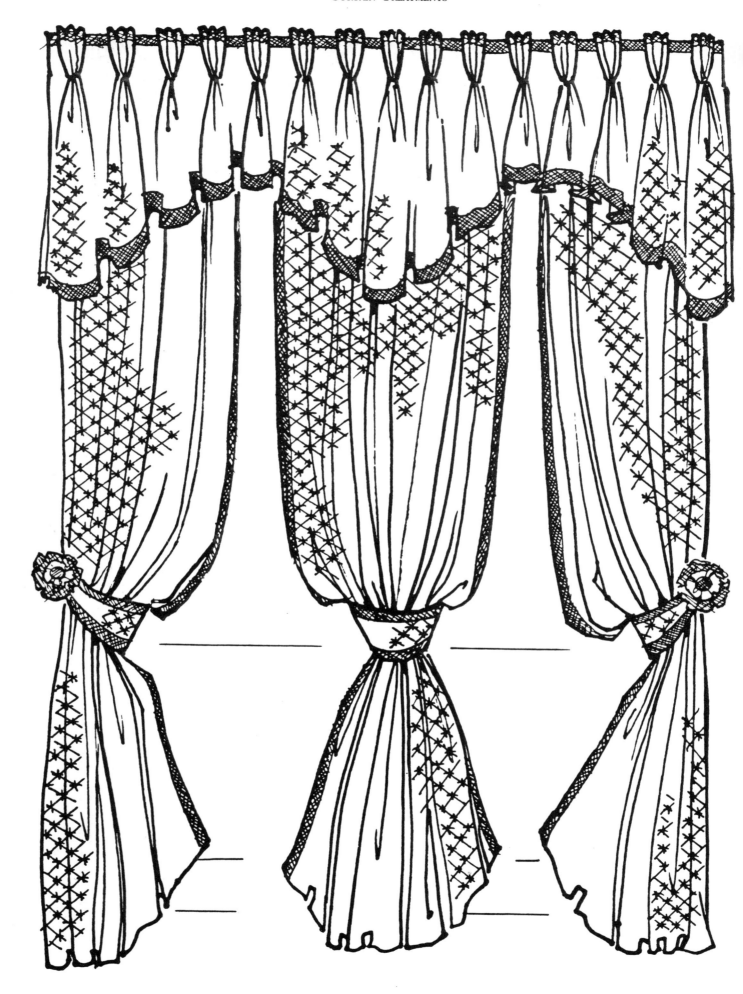

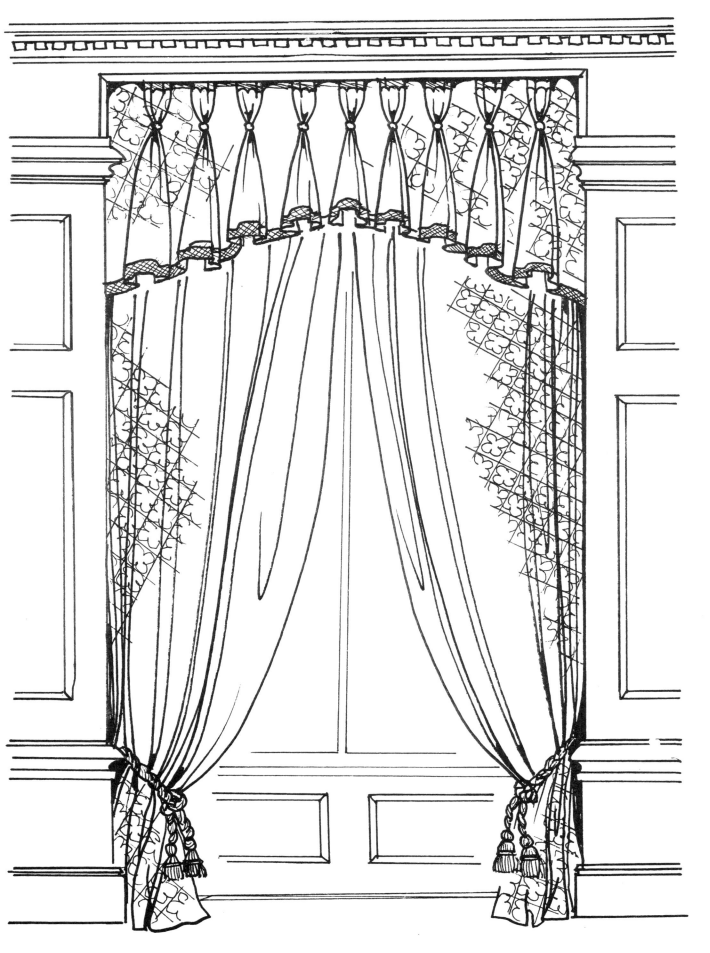

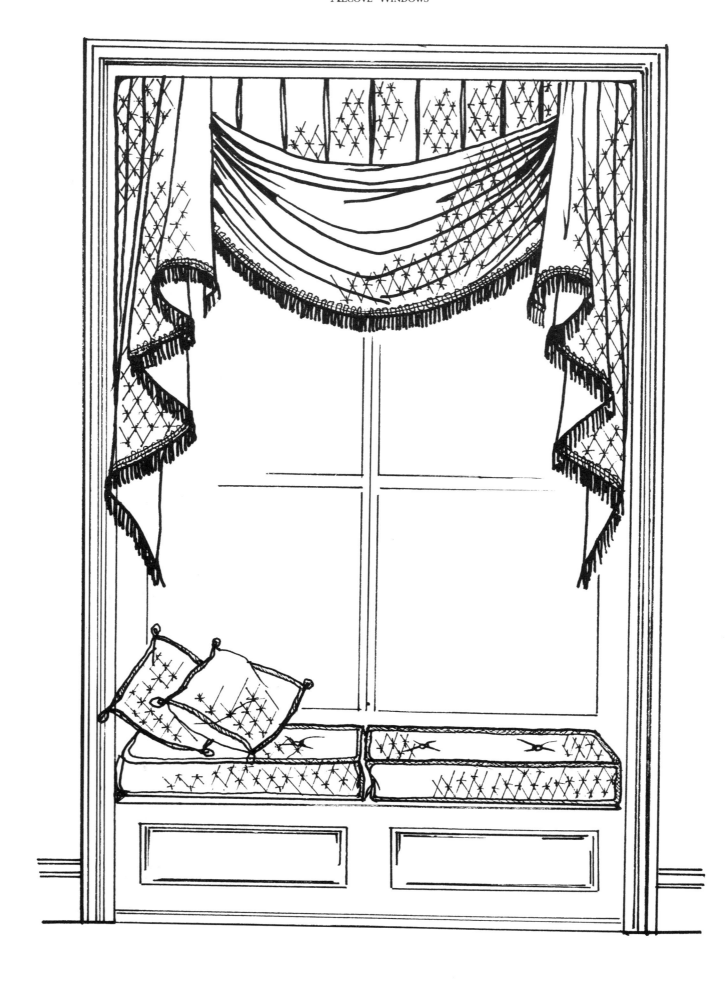

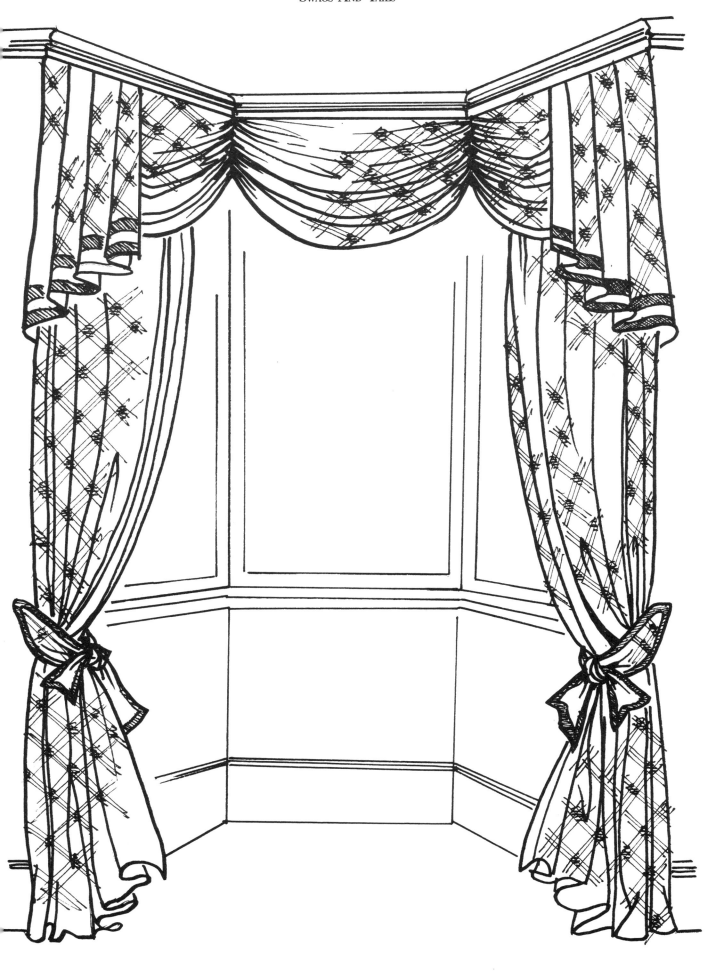

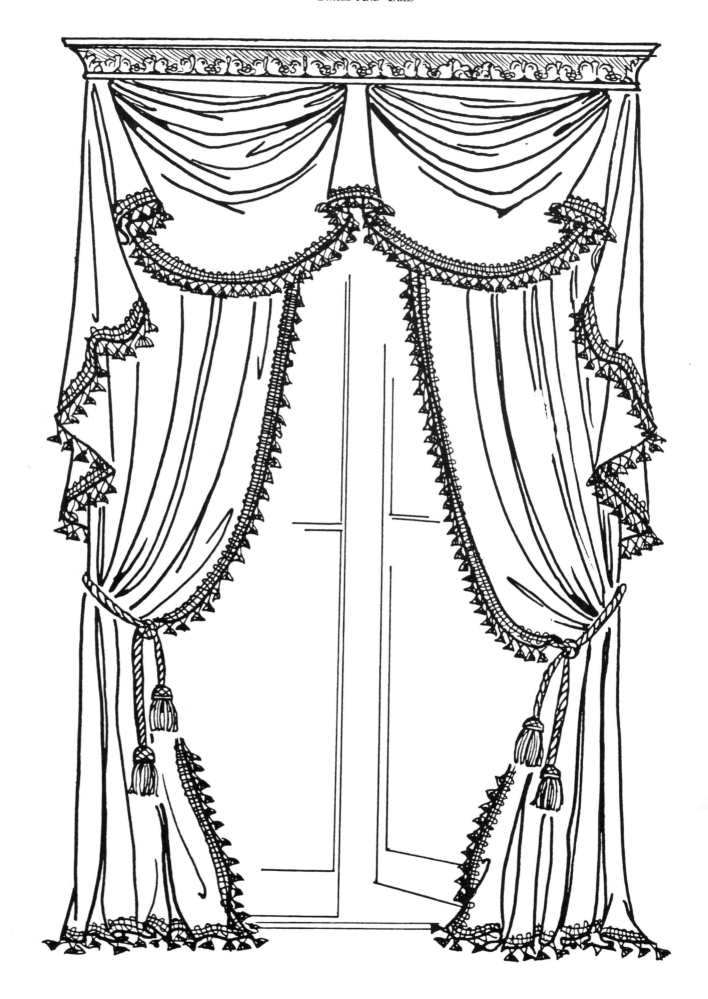

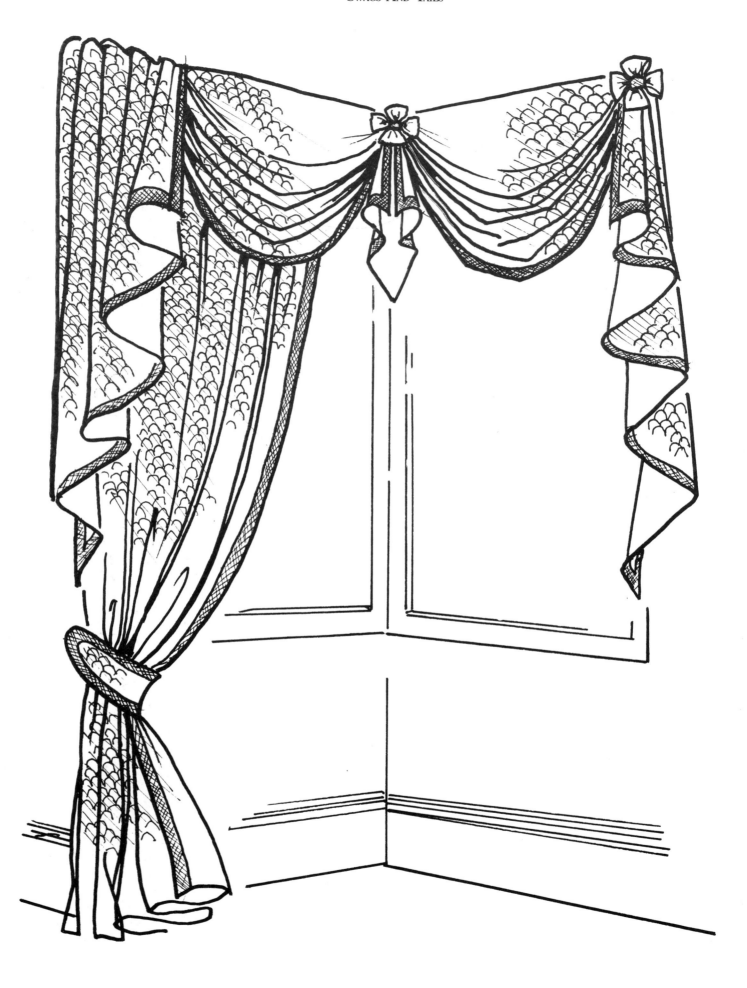

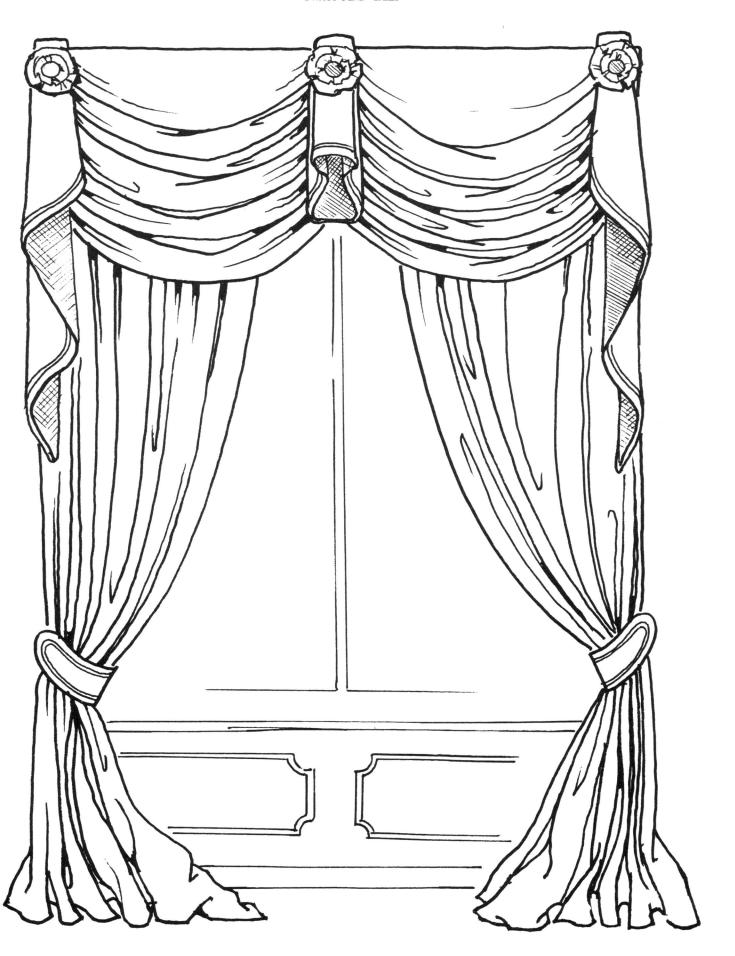

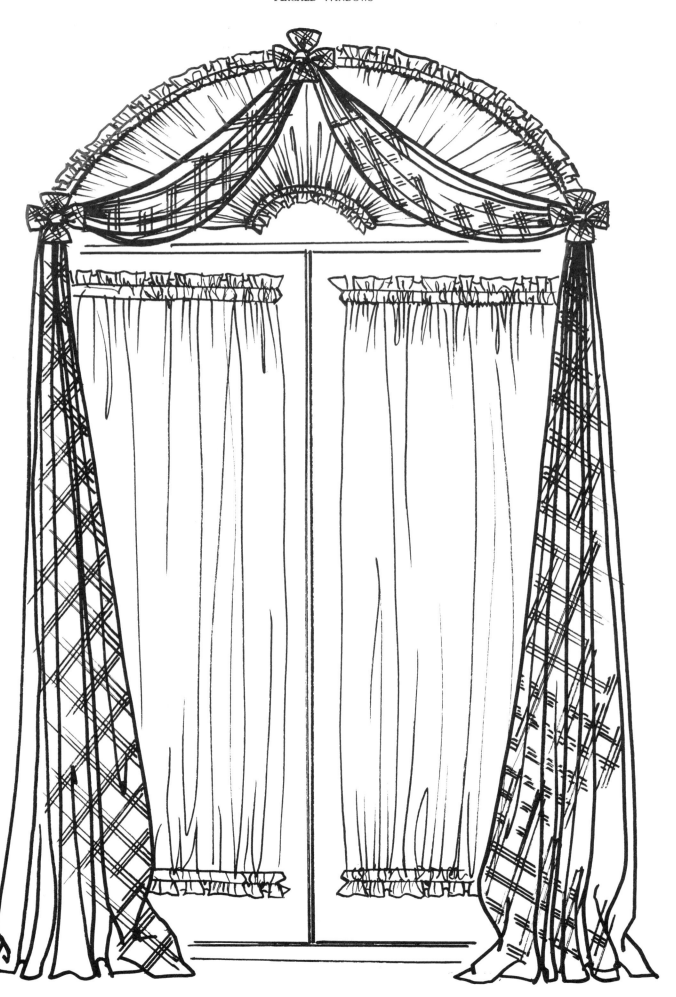

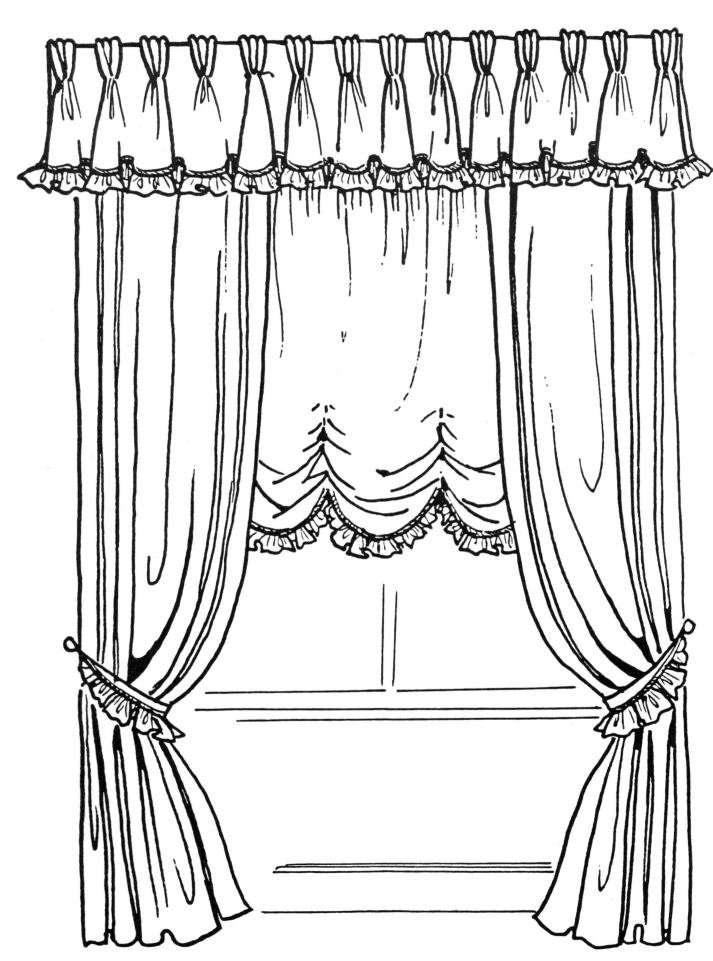

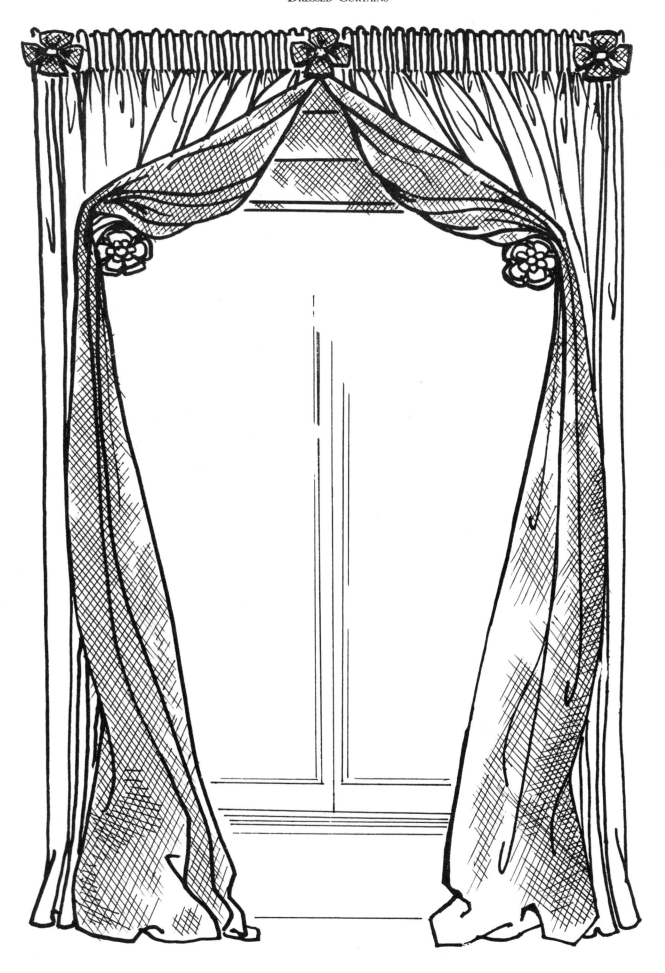

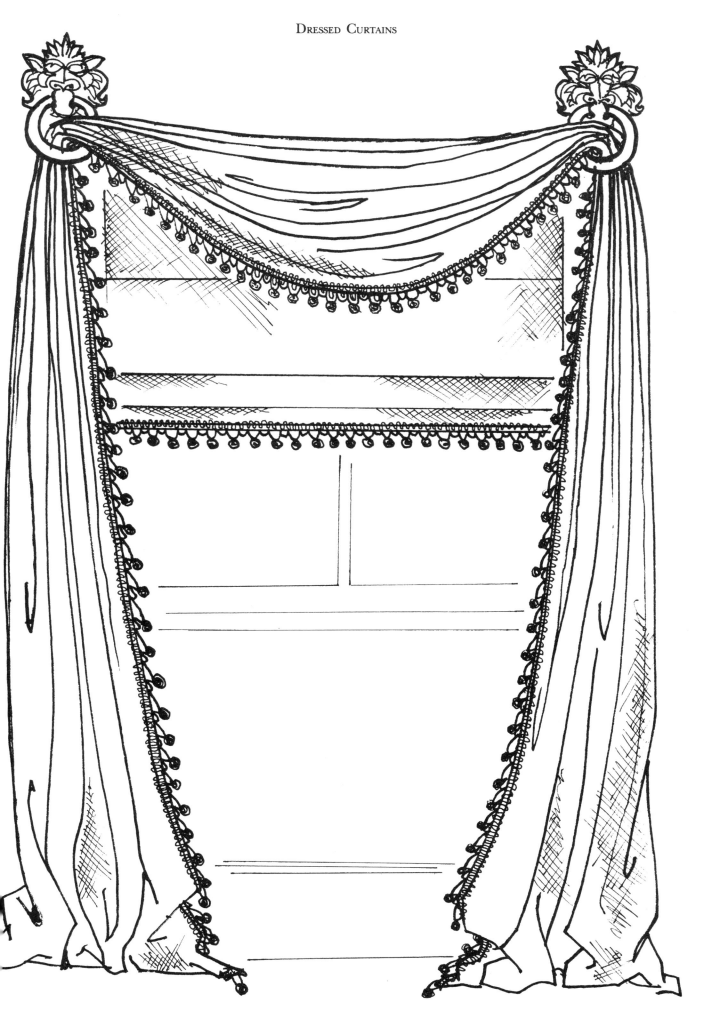

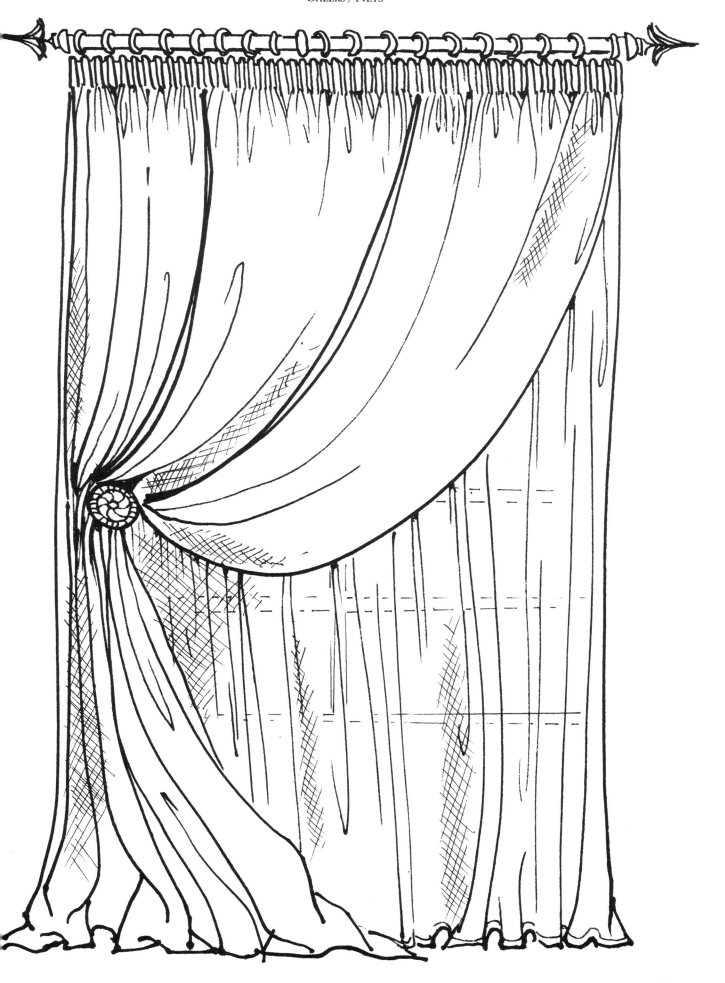

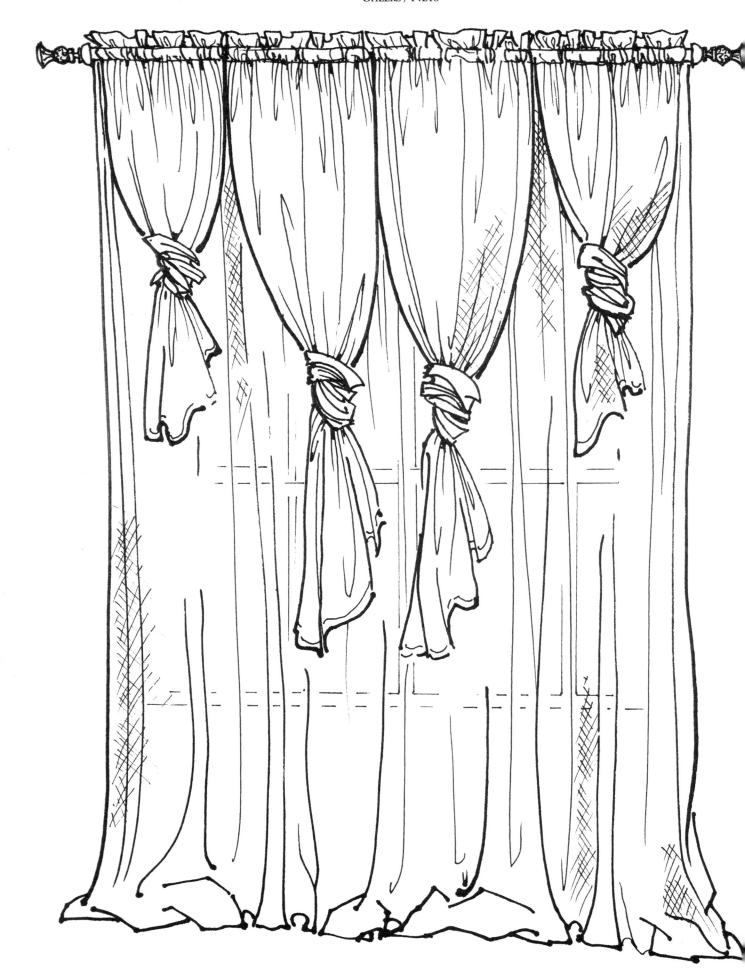

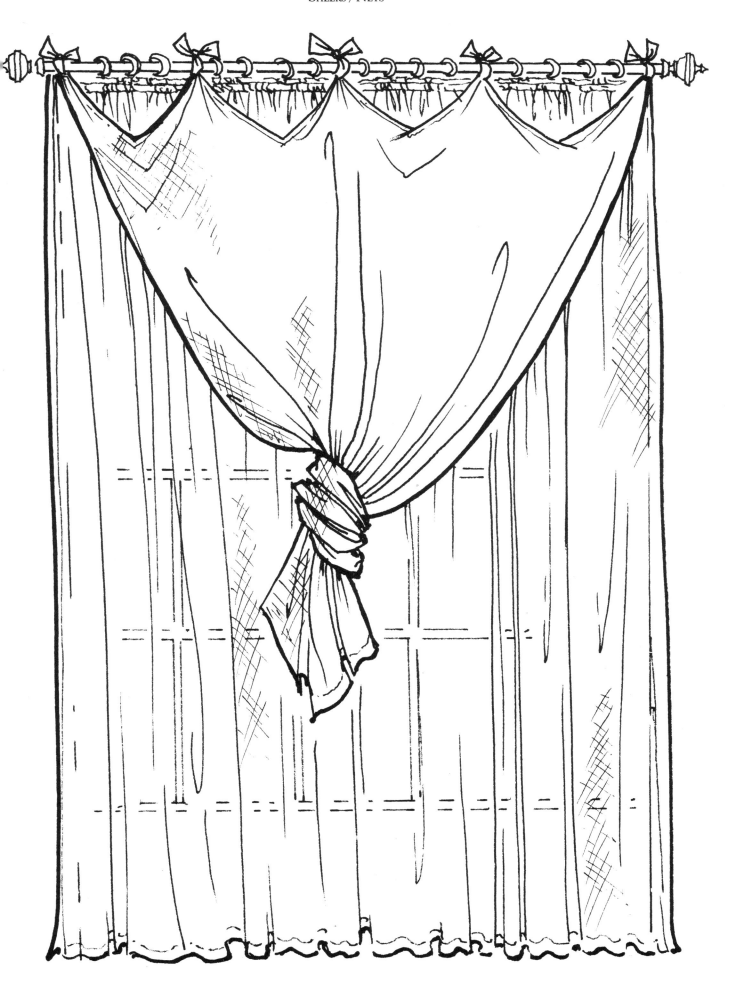

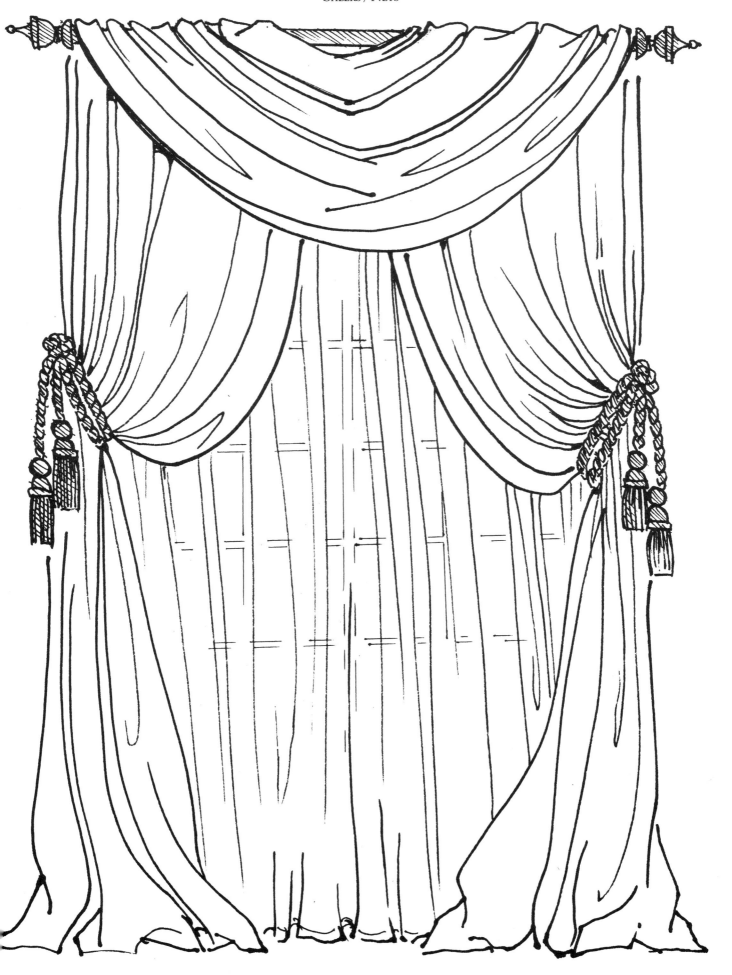

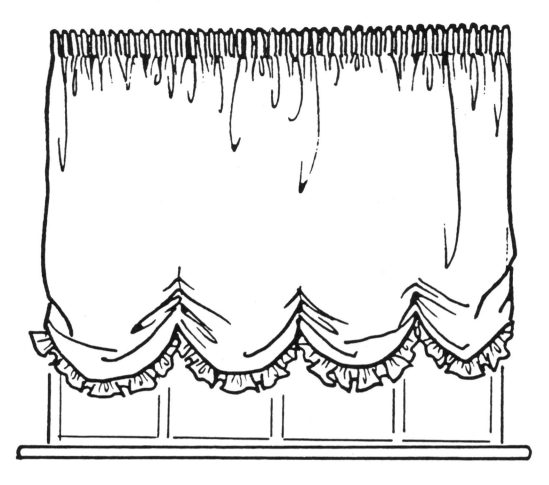

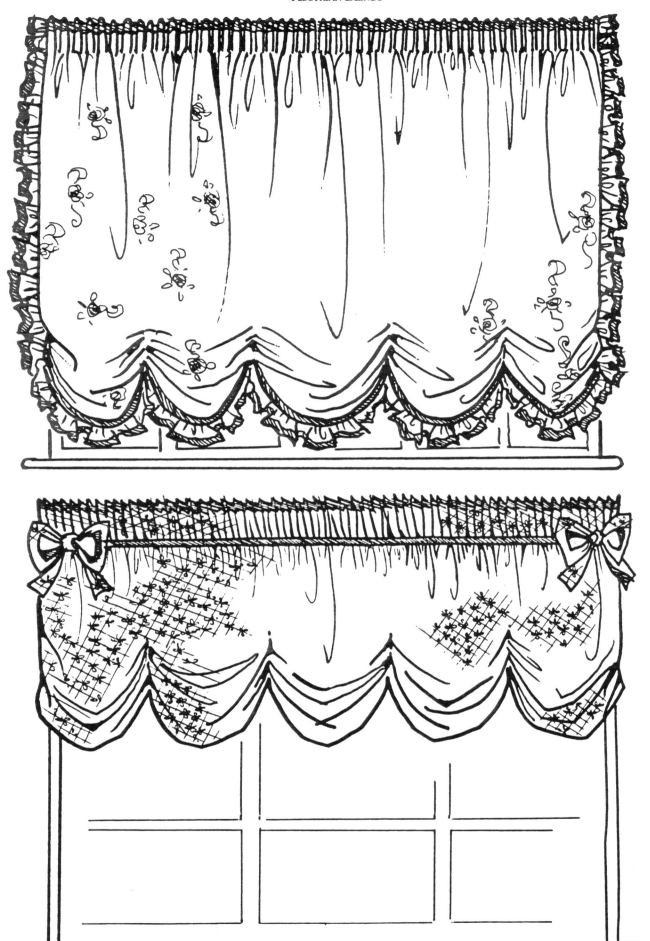

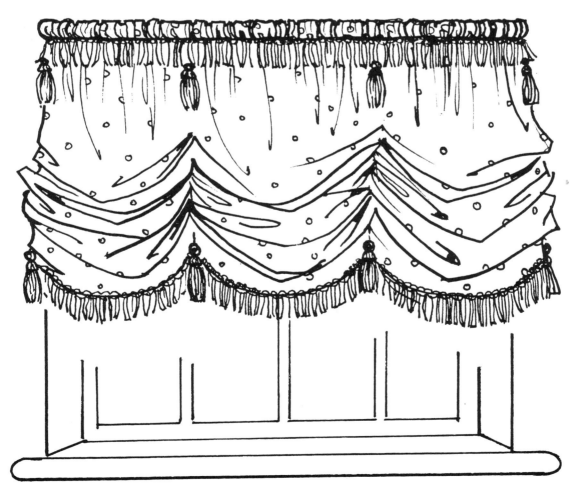

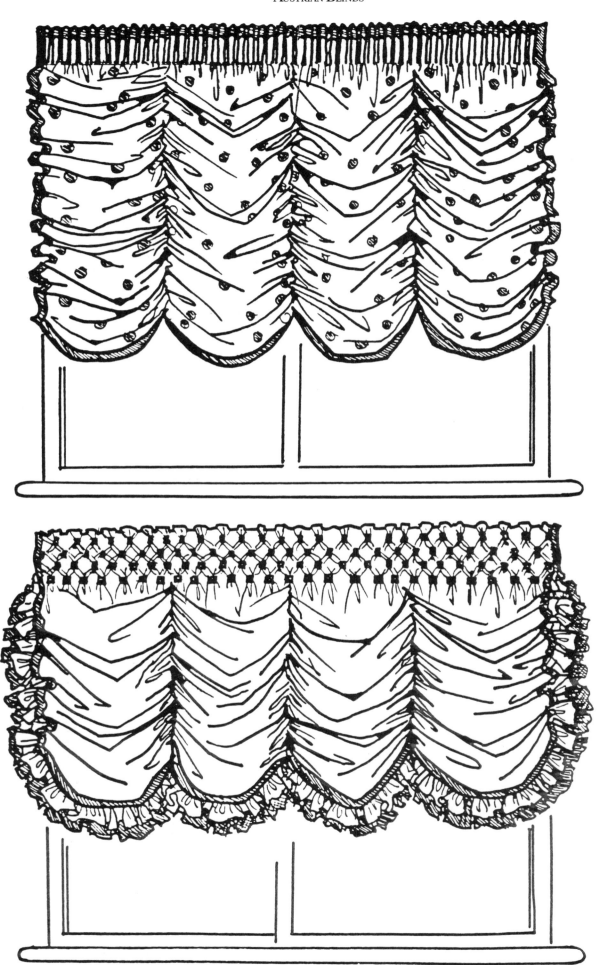

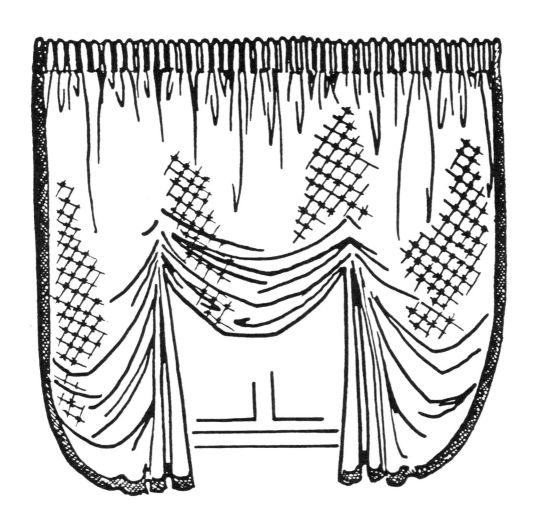

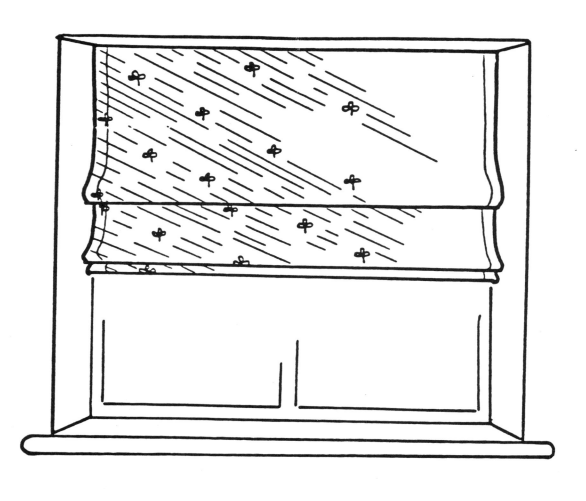

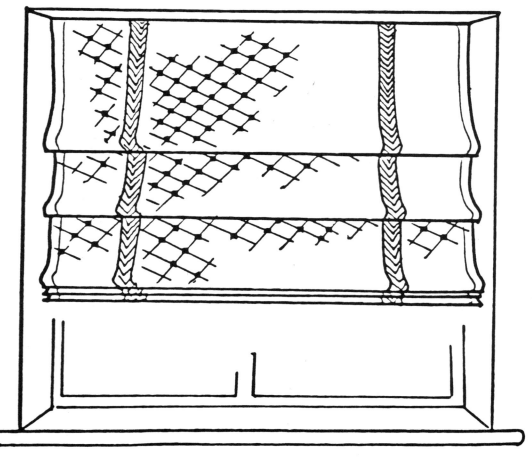

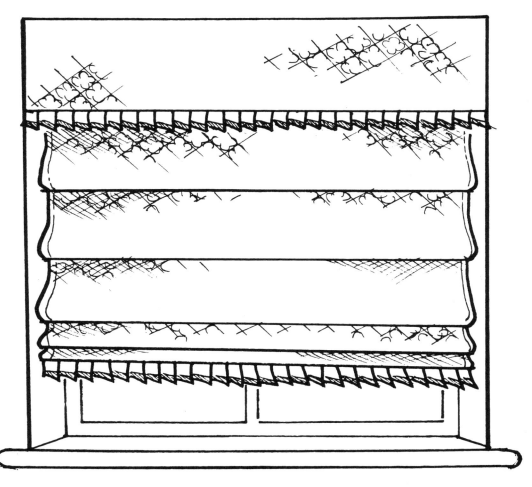

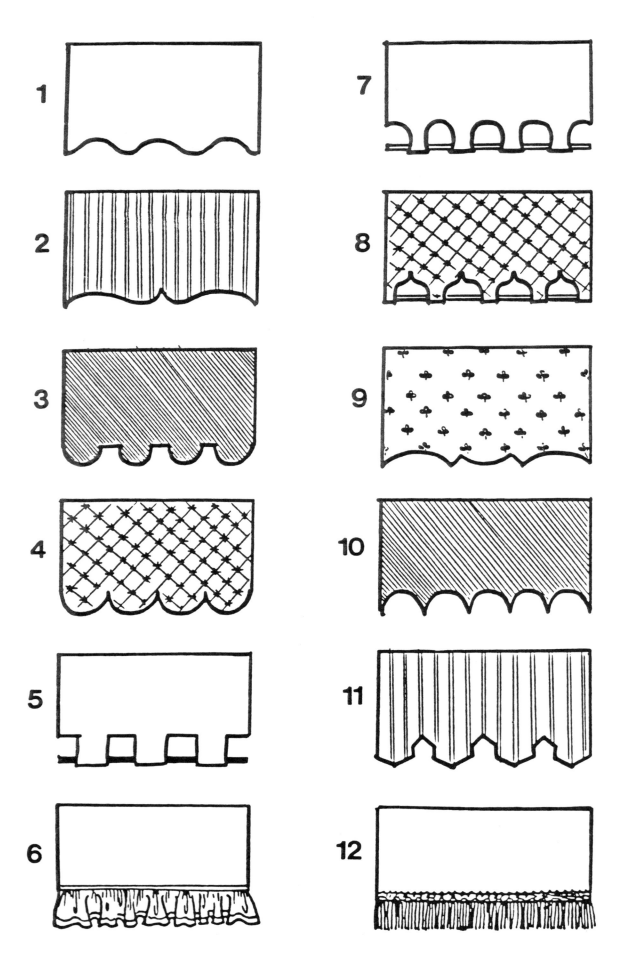

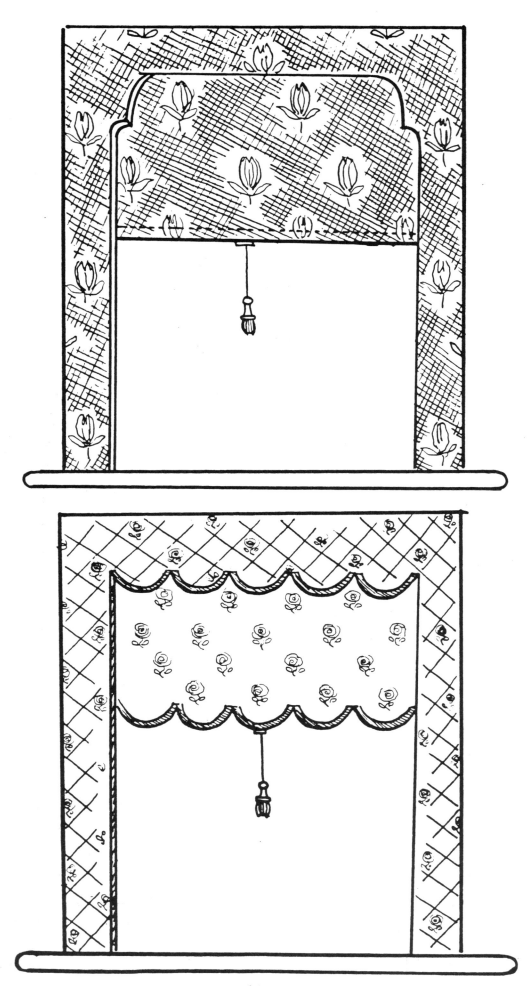

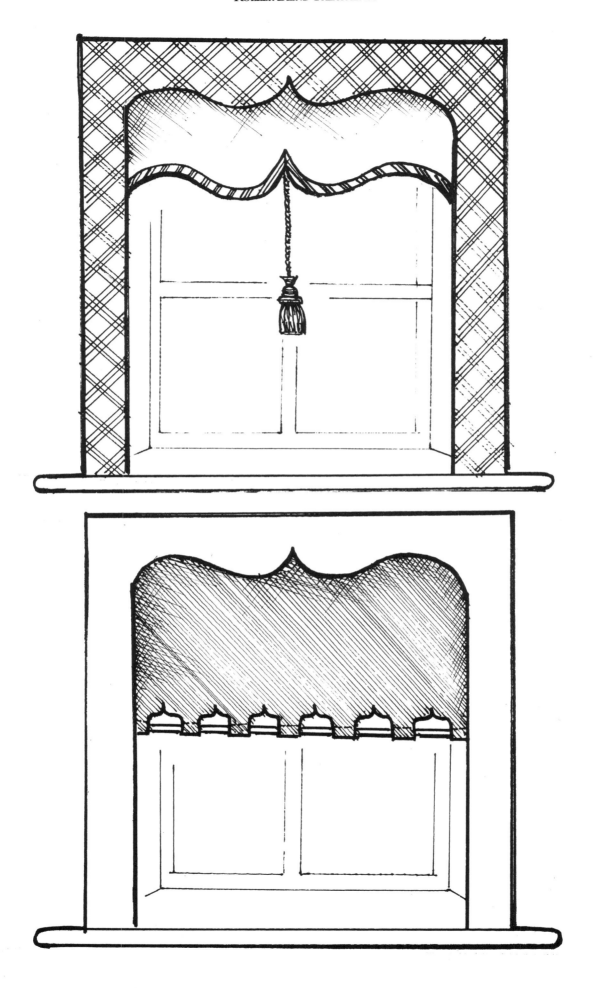

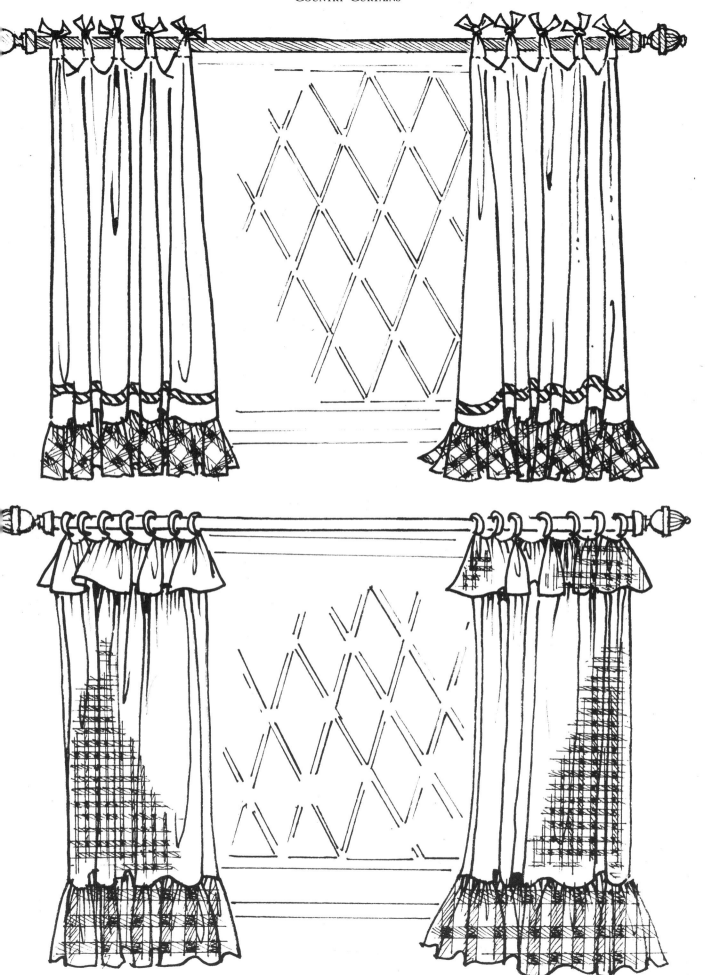

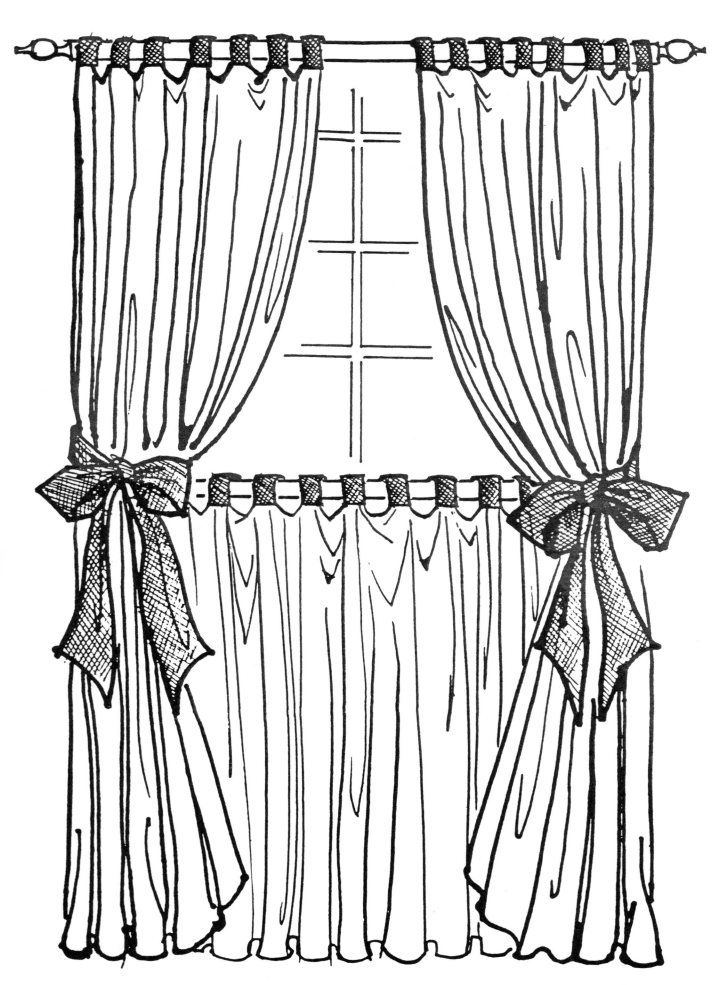

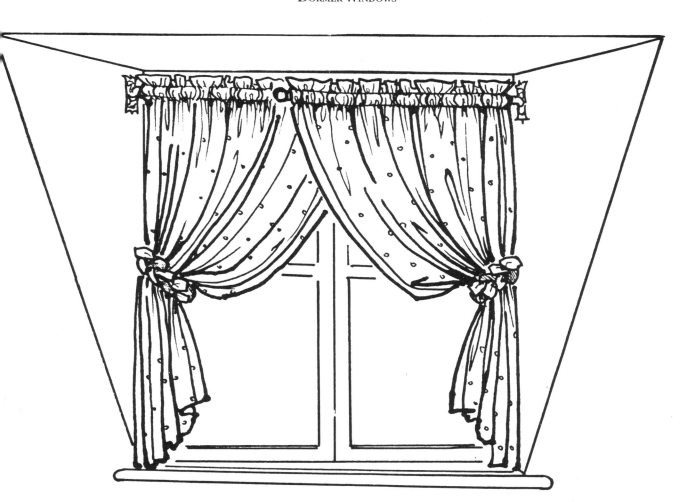

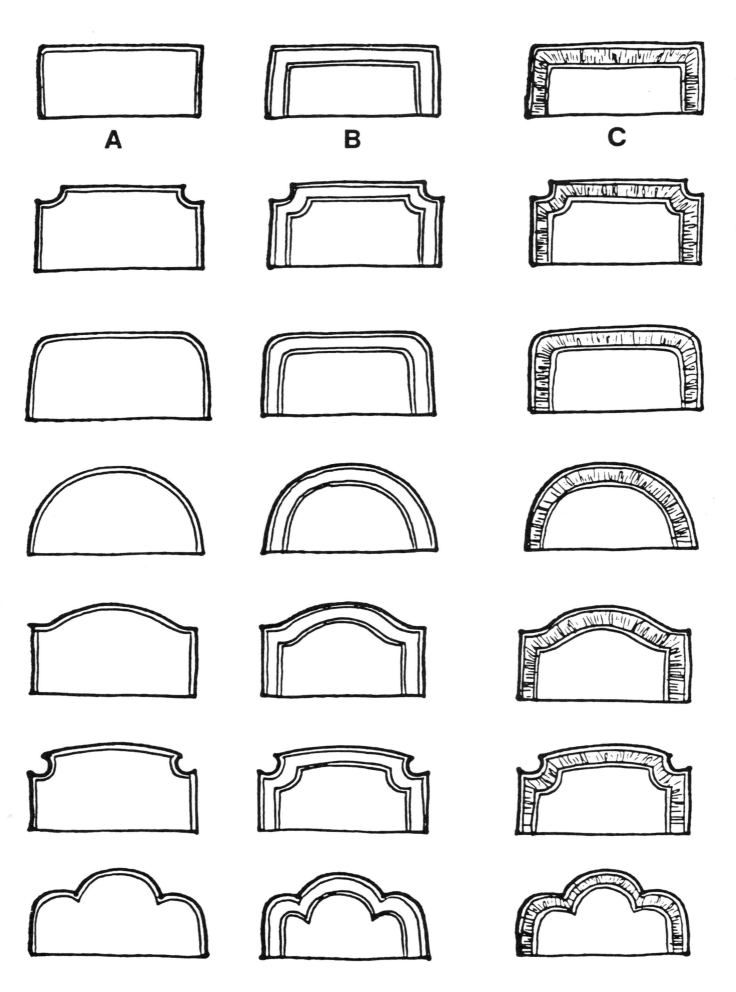

**A**                    **B**                    **C**

# BED COVERS

THROWOVER

OUTLINE STITCH

RANDOM STITCH

FRILLED

PADDED HEM

FRILLED VALANCE

BOX VALANCE

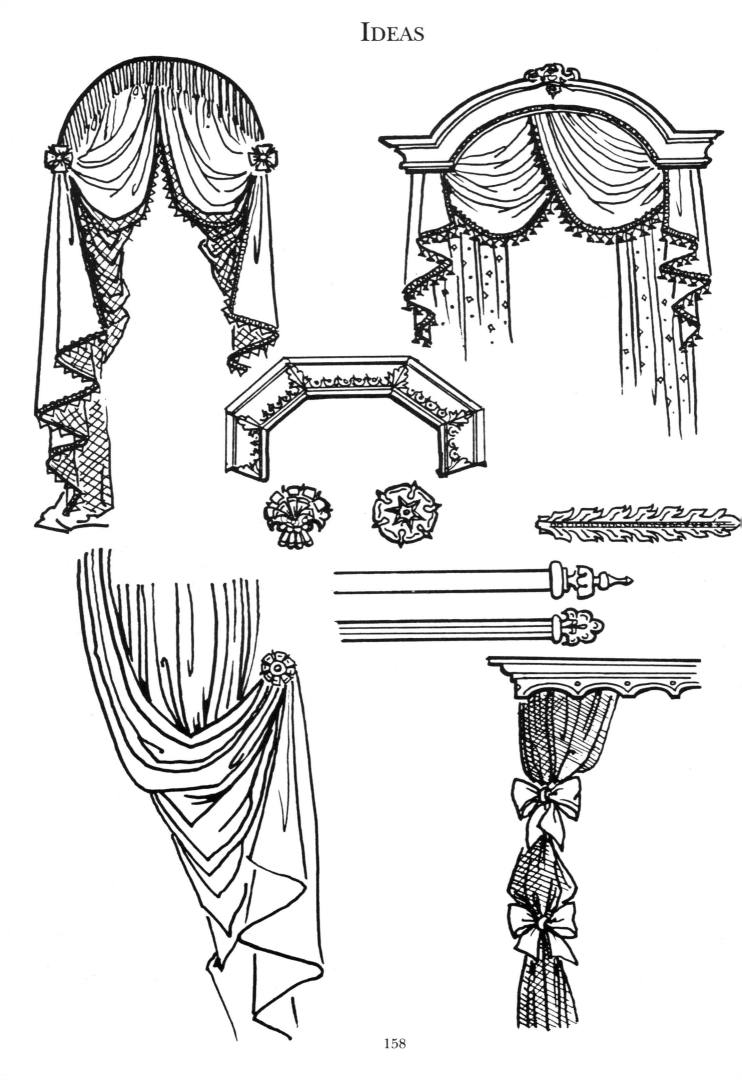

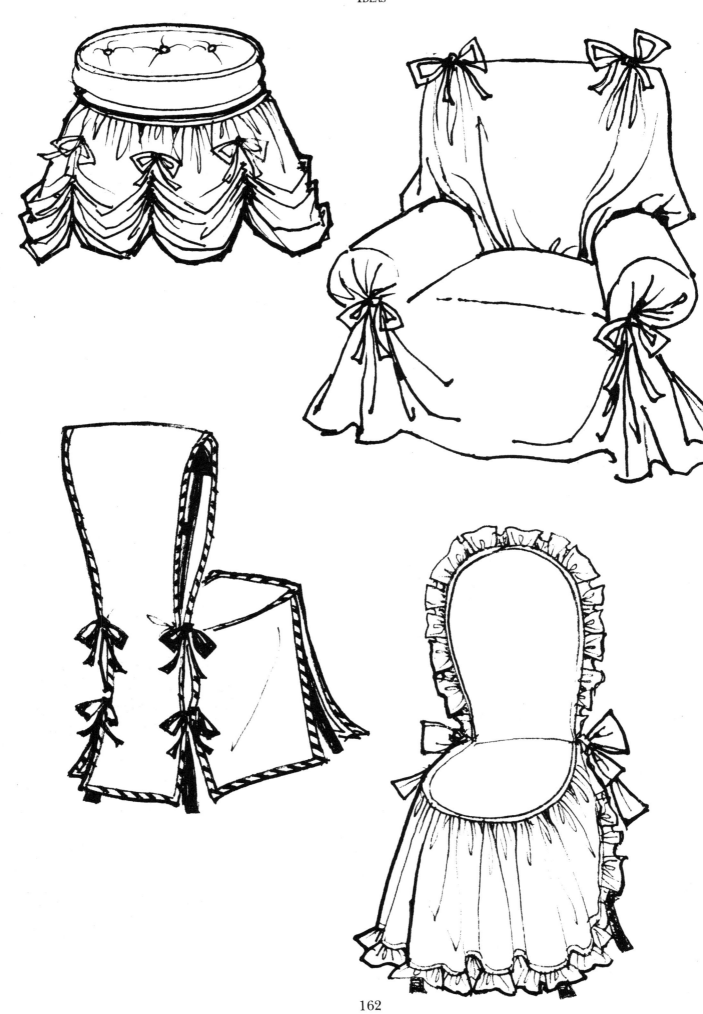

# SUPPLIERS U.K.

## FABRICS

G.P. & J. BAKER LTD
P.O. BOX 30
WEST END ROAD
HIGH WYCOMBE
BUCKS HP11 2QD
TEL:   01494   471166
FAX:   01494   474771
(General fabrics, plain and print)

JANE CHURCHILL
151 SLOANE STREET
LONDON  SW1X  9BZ
TEL:  0171  730  637

COLEFAX & FOWLER
HEAD OFFICE
118 GARRATT LANE
LONDON  SW18  4DG
TEL:  0171  730  9847
FAX:  0171  259  9189

SHOP
110  FULHAM ROAD
LONDON  SW3  6RL
TEL:  0171  373  7916

DESIGNERS GUILD
277 KINGS ROAD
LONDON  SW3  5EN
TEL:  0171  351  5775
FAX:  0171  243  7710

DECORATIVE FABRICS
GALLERY
278 - 280 BROMPTON ROAD
LONDON  SW3  2AS
TEL:  0171  589  4778
FAX:  0171  589  4781

THE DESIGN ARCHIVES
10 - 12 WHARFDALE ROAD
BOURNMOUTH
DORSET  BH4  9BT
TEL:  01202  753248
FAX:  01202  764256

ANNA FRENCH
HEAD OFFICE
108 SHAKESPEAR ROAD
LONDON  SW2  0QQ
TEL:  0171  737  6555
FAX:  0171  274  8913

SHOP
343 KINGS ROAD
LONDON  SW3  5ES
TEL:  0171  351  112

MONKWELL FABRICS
HEAD OFFICE
10 - 12 WHARFDALE ROAD
BOURNMOUTH
DORSET  BH4  9BT
TEL:  01202  752944
FAX:  01202  762582

OSBOURNE AND LITTLE
HEAD OFFICE
49 TEMPERLEY ROAD
LONDON  SW12  8QE
TEL:  0181  675 2255
FAX :  0181  673 8254

SHOP
304 KINGS ROAD
LONDON  SW3  5UH
TEL:  0171  352 1456
(Fabrics and trimmings)

BERNARD THORPE
6 BURNSALL STREET
LONDON  SW3  3SR
TEL:  0171  352  5745
FAX:  0171  376  3640
(Fabrics printed in own colours)

BRIAN YATES
3 RIVERSIDE PARK
CANTON ROAD
LANCASTER  LA1  3TE
TEL:  01524  35035
FAX:  01524  32232

SHOP
G26 DESIGN CENTRE
CHELSEA HARBOUR
LONDON  SW10  0XE
TEL:  0171  352  0123

## BLINDS (SHADES)

BLIND FASHION
UNIT 8
TREADWAY TECHNICAL CENTER
LOUDWATER
HIGHWYCOMBE
BUCKS HP10 9RS
TEL:  01628  529676
FAX:  01628  521684

HUNTER  DOUGLAS
INDUSTRIAL EATATE
LARKHALL
SCOTLAND  ML9  2PD
TEL:  01698  88777
(Metal Blinds)

## SHEERS/NETS/VOILES

JAB INTERNATIONAL
15 - 19 CAVENDISH PLACE
LONDON  W1M  9DL
TEL:  0171  636  1343
FAX:  0171  436  2412
(Also lots of Furnishing Fabrics)

HILL  AND KNOWEL
13 MOUNT STREET
FELTHAM
MIDDLESEX  TW13  6AR
TEL:  0181  893  3334
FAX:  0181  893  3850

CELIA BRITWELL
17 WESTBOURNE PARK ROAD
LONDON  W2  5QH
TEL:  0171  221  0877
FAX:  0171  229  7673

## LININGS

PORTER NICHOLSON
NORLINGTON ROAD
LONDON  EC10  6JX
TEL:  0181  539  6106
FAX:  0181  558  9200
(Coloured Linings)

F.R.STREET LTD
FREDRICK HOUSE
HURRICANE WAY
WICKFORD BUSINESS PARK
WICKFORD
ESSEX  SS11  8YB
TEL:  01268  766677
FAX:  01268  764534

## TRIMMINGS

WENDY  CUSHING
HEAD OFFICE
UNIT 8-9
ORIENT INDUSTRIAL PARK
SIMONDS ROAD
LEYTON
LONDON  E10  7DE
TEL:  0181  556  3555
FAX:  0181  558  6883

SHOP
UNIT G7
DESIGN CENTRE
CHELSEA HARBOUR
LONDON  SW10  0XE
TEL:  0171  351  5796

WEMYSS HOULES
40 NEWMAN STREET
LONDON  W1P  3PA
TEL:  0171  255  3305
FAX:  0171  580  9420

TURNELL AND GIGON
UNIT M20
DESIGN CENTRE
CHELSEA HARBOUR
LONDON  SW10  0XE
TEL:  0171  351  5142
FAX:  0171  376  7945

HENRY NEWBURY
18 NEWMAN STREET
LONDON  W1P  4AB
TEL:  0171  636  2053
FAX:  0171  436  6406
(INEXPENSIVE)

JOHN LEWIS  (DEPT STORE)
278-306 OXFORD STREET
LONDON  W1A  1EX
TEL:  0171  629  7711
FAX:  0171  629  0849
(Poles and Trimmings, inexpensive)

Phone the above number to find the
location of your nearest John Lewis
partnership store.

## TRACKING/POLES/
## ACCESSORIES

COPE AND TIMMINS
ANGEL ROAD WORKS
EDMONTON
LONDON  N18  3AY
TEL:  0181  803  6481
FAX:  0181  884  2322

HUNTER AND HYLAND
201 - 205 KINGSTON ROAD
LEATHERHEAD
SURREY  KT22  7PB
TEL:  01372  378511
FAX:  01372  370038

McKINNEY & CO
1 WANDON ROAD
LONDON  SW6  2JF
TEL:  0171  384  1377
FAX:  0171  736  1196

JOHN LEWIS  (DEPT STORE)
(See Under Trimmings)

## HEADBOARDS/
## CUSHIONS/
## TABLECLOTHS

WENDY BAKER AND ASSOCIATES
THE OLD MALTHOUSE
HAM
MARLBOROUGH SN8 3RB
TEL:  01488  668989
FAX:  01488  668818

IT IS WELL WORTH A VISIT TO
THE DESIGN CENTRE,
CHELSEA HARBOUR
LONDON SW10
WHERE NUMEROUS COMPANIES
NOW HAVE SHOWROOMS.

# SUPPLIERS U.S.A.

## FABRICS

BRUNSCHWIG & FILS,
979 3rd Avenue, N.Y.C.,
NY 10022.
TEL: (212) 838 7878

CLARENCE HOUSE,
(Expensive)
979 3rd Avenue, N.Y.C.,
NY 10022.
TEL: (212) 752 2890

JACK LENOR LARSON,
(Georgous)
232 East 59th Street, N.Y.C.,
NY
TEL: (212) 674 3993

SCALAMANDRE,
950 3rd Avenue, N.Y.C.,
NY 10022
TEL: (212) 415 3900

SCHUMACHER,
(Huge collection, all prices, all
types, including trimmings)
939 3rd Avenue, N.Y.C.,
NY 10022.
TEL: (212) 415 3900

COWTAN AND TOUT,
979 3rd Avenue, N.Y.C.,
NY 10022.
TEL: (212) 753 4488

OSBOURNE AND LITTLE,
65 Commerce Road,
Stamford,
CT 06902.
(Head Office. Will give you
addresses throughout U.S.A.)

## LININGS

DESIGNTEX,
(800) 237 236

MILLIKEN,
(212) 819 4338
(Represented in all large towns
- specialists in anti cold linings &
wind resistant)

## SHEERS

HINSON & CO.,
979 3rd Avenue, N.Y.C.,
NY 10022.
TEL: (212) 688 5538

GIGI INTERIORS LTD.,
170 South Main Street,
Yardley,
PA 19067.
TEL: (215) 493 8052

## TRIMMINGS

SCUMACHER,
939 3rd Avenue, N.Y.C.,
NY 10022.
TEL: (212) 415 3900

M&J TRIMMINGS,
1008 6th Avenue, N.Y.C.,
NY 10018.
TEL: (212) 391 9072

FABRIC CENTER,
485 Electric Avenue,
P.O. Box 8212,
Fitchburg,
MA 01420-8212.
TEL: (508) 343 4402
(Send for catalogue - Fabrics,
Trims, Poles etc.)

## TRACKING SYSTEMS & POLES

KIRSCH,
P.O. Box 370,
Sturgis,
MI 49091.
TEL: (800) 528 1407
(Throughout the U.S. Call for your
nearest branch)

BALI/GRABER,
P.O. Box 500,
Momtgomery,
PA 17752.
TEL: (800) 544 4749
(Throughout the U.S. Call for
your nearest branch)

JANOVIC PLAZA,
1150 Third Avenue
New York.
NY 10021
TEL: (212) 772 1400
FAX: (212) 249 0608
(Store selling all lines of window
hardware)

GRAPER DRAPERY,
HARDWARE,
Middleton,
WI 53562.
TEL: (800) 356 9102

## HEADBOARDS

HAMILTON FURNITURE,
107 East 63rd Street, N.Y.C.,
NY 10021.
TEL: (212) 826 0826

## PLEATING

SF PLEATING,
61 Green Point Avenue,
Brooklyn,
NY 11222.
TEL: (718) 383 7950